I would like to dedicate this book to my children Stephanie, Maxson, and Carianna, as well as my partner, Dr. Lissa Joy Geiken, for providing balance, love, and caring during the writing process.

Michael Doyle

Table of Contents

What do you think of this book? We want to hear from you!

Microsoft is interested in hearing your feedback so we can continually improve our
books and learning resources for you. To participate in a brief online survey, please visit:

microsoft.com/learning/booksurvey

What do you think of this book? We want to hear from you!

Microsoft is interested in hearing your feedback so we can continually improve our
books and learning resources for you. To participate in a brief online survey, please visit:

microsoft.com/learning/booksurvey

Introduction

Welcome to *Microsoft® SharePoint® 2010: Customizing My Site*! The My Site component of Microsoft SharePoint has been around for a long time (since SharePoint 2003), but it has only recently caught the attention of the greater SharePoint community. The explosion of social networking has made the My Site component one of the key pieces in creating a cohesive SharePoint solution. Straight out of the box, the My Site component is quite powerful, but it is far from easy to customize. When I first started customizing the My Site interface several years ago, there was basically nothing on the Internet or in the bookstores to help me, so I had to do things the hard way. Hoping to help others to avoid my pains, I started blogging and speaking about how to customize the My Site Host. This went on for a while, until I decided that there needed to be a more comprehensive piece of work out there for people to have so that they can see what is possible and be empowered to make changes for themselves. This led to the creation of this book. It is my hope that the contents within will help guide you on your way to personalizing the My Site Host to fit the business needs of your organization. When it comes down to it, the whole goal is to for users to be enabled and focus on the business needs rather than on how to use the technology.

Who Should Read This Book

This book is intended for a wide audience. The My Site Host covers too many aspects of SharePoint to be pinned down to one or two particular roles. A proper implementation of My Sites affects administrators, developers, managers, engineers, and pretty much anyone that deals with personal information. That being said, the bulk of the content of this book would come under the SharePoint administrator's realm with another large section aimed at designers. There are some sections that are more developer oriented. The point to be made here is that it takes a wide range of skills to customize the My Site Host (and personalization sites beneath) and almost anyone connected with My Sites would benefit from reading parts of this book to get a better idea of how it all fits together and what is possible. Although it is possible to do almost anything, given enough time and resources, I hope this book will give readers some insight into what they can change with the resources they have available and realize the largest return on their investment of time and money.

Assumptions

Microsoft SharePoint 2010: Customizing My Site assumes some basic knowledge of SharePoint 2010 Enterprise edition, whether in the role of administrator, developer, designer, or architect. The concepts of User Profiles and Active Directory are fundamental to grasp most of the content contained within. Because this book covers a great many aspects of implementing the My Site host, it is likely that some section will not be relevant to your role, but it should at least provide some level of understanding because customization and/or implementation of My Sites concerns everyone connected to SharePoint.

Organization of this Book

Microsoft® SharePoint® 2010: Customizing My Site is generally divided into two main sections. The first part is focuses on how to get the My Site host set up and running correctly. The rest of the book looks at how to customize various parts of the functionality and social components. You can use this information to get an idea of what is involved in the creation and customization of a My Site Host. You can also use the book as a reference guide for when you have specific tasks that need to be accomplished. The chapters are described here.

Chapter 1   What's New in Microsoft SharePoint 2010 My Sites

SharePoint 2010 brought a host of new functionality to My Sites. Chapter 1 goes over the new functionality in brief detail and outlines some of the benefits. This is a good start to get a feel for what is coming in the rest of the book.

Chapter 2   The User Profile Service

Getting the User Profile Service running is the first step in creating the My Site. It is also one of the most challenging steps. Unlike SharePoint 2007, there are a lot of caveats involved, and doing it wrong can waste a lot of time, requiring you to delete the User Profile Service and start over. This chapter covers creating the User Profile Service, repairing it, working with profile pictures, and upgrading from SharePoint 2007.

Chapter 3   Setting Up My Sites

Chapter 3 describes creating a My Site Host and the decisions involved afterward, such as setting quotas on personalization sites and Trusted My Site Hosts. There is also a part on upgrading the look and feel from a SharePoint 2007 My Site.

Chapter 4   Multiple Farms and My Sites

Connecting multiple farms requires many very specific steps. There are two methods that can be used. You can consume a central farm's User Profile Service or you can replicate User Profile data between farms. This chapter shows both ways and why you would choose one over the other.

Chapter 5   Customizing My Site Navigation

Modifying the navigation of a My Site Host is a lot more complicated than a regular SharePoint site. There are multiple levels of navigation and additional components to worry about such as audience-based Personalization sites. Chapter 5 covers the various navigation elements and how to customize them to fit your needs.

Chapter 6   Modifying the My Site Host

The My Site Host appears as a single page with multiple tabs, but it is actually multiple pages in multiple locations. This presents difficulty when attempting to customize the pages. This chapter addresses how and why to customize the pages so they can be branded to fit the needs of your organization.

Chapter 7   Organizational Charts

There isn't a lot that can be modified with Organizational Charts, but this chapter describes what you can do. It also covers the redundancy of the various Organizational Charts and how some of that space can be regained.

Chapter 8   Tags and Notes

Tags and notes are two new features in SharePoint, which are tied to the My Site Host. These social components present some new issues in both training and customization. This chapter focuses on turning them on and off as well as managing them.

Chapter 9   Site Membership

Site Membership shows which SharePoint sites a person has been added to individually. There are some issues with how individuals are added. The chapter shows you how to modify the page in SharePoint Designer.

Chapter 10   Colleagues

This chapter focuses on the emails that are sent about adding colleagues, and explains how to control them.

Chapter 11   Profile Properties

There is a lot to consider when creating and using profile properties. Chapter 11 covers the options available and how to use them. It also shows an example of how to use profile properties to provide a customized Twitter feed on a person's My Site About Me page.

Chapter 12   People Search

The people search page really shows the power of properly populated User Profile properties. This chapter shows you how to customize the people search page by showing how to customize the refinement panel and the results. This is a challenging topic but can yield impressive results to the end user. It also shows how to improve accuracy and add counts.

Chapter 13   Outlook Integration

Chapter 13 focuses on the Outlook Social Connector that hooks into the My Site Host, enabling items to be shown from the newsfeed. It also shows how to get pictures from My Sites into Outlook by exporting them into Active Directory.

Chapter 14   Personal Sites

Personal sites provide an interesting challenge to the administrator of the SharePoint farm because every personal site is its own site collection. This chapter shows how to maintain consistent master pages across all these site collections as well as some general guidelines about how to deal with the difficulties of managing personal sites.

Code Samples

All the My Site code examples shown in the book can be found at the following address:

http://go.microsoft.com/FWLink/?Linkid=227896

The code examples are text (.txt) files and organized by chapter. We've also provided all the code examples in a Word document for your convenience.

Acknowledgments

I have a multitude of people to thank for this book. It has developed over the years through experience and a desire to share my challenges and successes with others. It wasn't easy, but it made me realize how much time and effort it takes to make books like these possible. This is the natural culmination of years of blogging, speaking, and answering questions on forums. Every question that was asked, every person I helped, and every hurdle I overcame (often with help from others) led to the book that you have before you.

I have to thank Microsoft Press, O'Reilly Media, Ken Brown, Joy Earles, and all the other people who helped hone this book and make it a reality. Without them this book would not have been possible. Thanks for the guidance, the reviewing, and the polishing that was both desired and needed.

Errata & Book Support

We've made every effort to ensure the accuracy of this book and its companion content. Any errors that have been reported since this book was published are listed on our Microsoft Press site at oreilly.com:

http://go.microsoft.com/FWLink/?Linkid=227895

If you find an error that is not already listed, you can report it to us through the same page.

If you need additional support, email Microsoft Press Book Support at mspinput@microsoft.com.

Please note that product support for Microsoft software is not offered through the addresses above.

We Want to Hear from You

At Microsoft Press, your satisfaction is our top priority and your feedback our most valuable asset. Please tell us what you think of this book at

http://www.microsoft.com/learning/booksurvey

The survey is short, and we read every one of your comments and ideas. Thanks in advance for your input!

Stay in Touch

Let's keep the conversation going! We're on Twitter: *http://twitter.com/MicrosoftPress*

Chapter 1
What's New in Microsoft SharePoint 2010 My Sites?

My Sites have undergone a major transformation since Microsoft SharePoint 2007. In conjunction with the surge of social computing worldwide, these changes have propelled companies to rethink how SharePoint works in their environment. Organizations want to capture the enthusiasm behind social computing and provide mechanisms for users to connect with each other while at the same time giving them a space to call their own. Not only does this give users a sense of community, it brings real value by providing a forum in which users can share ideas, documents, notes, tags, and changes in personal information.

Why Modify My Sites?

The first and most obvious reason to modify My Sites is to maintain the branded look and feel of your organization. A wide range of effort can go into branding, depending on how tailored you want it to be. A very simple but effective way is to simply change the colors and fonts. You can do this through the use of Themes, which is a new feature in SharePoint 2010. Any customization beyond Themes is likely to involve some serious expeditions into cascading style sheets (CSS) and Microsoft .NET code page modifications, which will take considerably more effort and time. This is in part because SharePoint branding requires a specialized skill set. More important, it's due to the nature of My Site, which is a combination of both a top-level site collection (with some files that can be modified with SharePoint Designer 2010 and some that cannot) and a personal site collection, for which each individual is their own site collection administrator.

The second reason to modify My Sites—which I think is the most important one—is to make the My Site host meet your business needs. You can remove the pieces that don't bring business value and add additional features such as custom profile properties and social media tie-ins that bring business value to your particular implementation. Once you have determined which pieces you use, you can get in and start further modification on the parts you plan to implement. Personalization sites might also be targeted toward specific groups of users, such as managers, new employees, or contractors. The end result should be something that people find easy to use, such that it's worth the relatively small effort to contribute your information and the equally important task of keeping it fresh.

New Features

Several features are new to SharePoint 2010 My Sites. The focus behind these new features is a desire to help connect users and to harness the power of social computing. As you review these new features, you might recognize some similar concepts in popular social networks; that similarity is quite intentional. By creating controls that people are familiar with, the amount of training required is substantially reduced. Let's take a brief look at these controls before we start getting too deep.

Tags

Tags are the new way to store your links. The basic concept of a tag is a word (or phrase) that is associated with a URL. These tags are grouped together in a tag cloud that is visible on your My Site (the tag cloud is just a Web Part that can be placed on any SharePoint site). For example, when you click the word "SharePoint" in the tag cloud, all the items with the tag "SharePoint" are displayed. Almost anything with a URL can be tagged. The Tags & Notes icon displays by default on every page in SharePoint. In Chapter 8, "Tags and Notes," you will see that users can even bookmark items that are not in SharePoint. The Tag Cloud Web Part need not be included on the My Site host to use tags, but you will need to place the cloud on another page in order for users to access their tags. Once a user has tagged content, she might see items in her newsfeed regarding content tagged by others with the same tag. This can be useful in gathering related links to content about a certain subject. This becomes even more powerful if all the users are using the same set of tags. But users are human, and without assistance, it is only natural that people will use multiple spellings or use different phrases or terminology to describe the same concept. To help bring order and establish some standardization, you can use the managed metadata term store in SharePoint. Although not specifically part of the My Site host, you will find that the term store is an extremely important part of making your My Site implementation more effective.

Note Board

The Note Board is an easy way to leave a message for an individual. If you browse to a person's profile, you will (by default) see a Note Board on which you can type anything you want, as shown in the following figure. The user will see the post the next time he visits his own profile page. He will also receive an email if the outgoing email has been configured to do so and he hasn't opted out of this service. Filtering of these notifications is not currently available; the only option is to get an email every time a person leaves a note or to not receive them at all.

Note Board

| |
| |

Post

◄Previous | Next►

Michael Doyle 8/27/2011 3:48 PM   Edit | Delete
Working on My Sites

A Note Board can be added to any SharePoint page, not just profile pages; thus, users can leave notes and comments on any page. This allows for immediate feedback, a particularly useful feature for project sites, document workspaces, and team sites.

Organizational Chart

One of the most graphically appealing additions to My Sites is the new Organizational Chart. With this Microsoft Silverlight tool, you can now browse through the hierarchy of your organization with ease. On one screen you can see your peers, your subordinates, your manager, and everyone directly above you, all the way to the top. You must have Silverlight installed on your computer to use this tool, but if you are going to be using SharePoint 2010, you are most likely going to want to use Silverlight, anyway. The addition of the new Silverlight Web Part to the list of available Web Parts in SharePoint 2010 means there will be an ever increasing number of Silverlight solutions. There isn't much you can do to modify how the Silverlight Organizational Chart is displayed, but there is an option to view an HTML version if your organization's policies prohibit the installation of Silverlight.

Themes

Just as with any other site, Themes (Microsoft Office Themes) can be used to quickly apply changes to the colors and fonts of both the My Site Host and an individual user's personalization site. Themes are easy to customize; the best tool to use is Microsoft PowerPoint 2010. Themes can be modified in SharePoint 2010, but PowerPoint offers many more customization options and its Create New Theme Colors dialog box is a much more intuitive user interface.

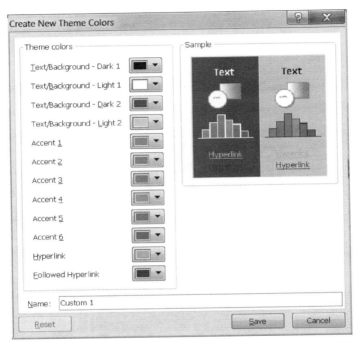

The dialog box provides a preview of how the colors will look. While this preview doesn't provide an exact rendering of how the theme will look in SharePoint, it does provide some insight. If your company has an existing PowerPoint deck that it uses as its template, you can use that to create an Office Theme. This will help you keep your company branding consistent. This practice doesn't replace custom branding, but it is a rather quick and easy way to put your stamp on how My Sites look. To create the Theme, simply save the PowerPoint presentation as an Office Theme. This will create a file with the .thmx extension, which you can then upload into the Themes gallery of your My Site Host or an individual personal site. Once there, you can apply it and modify it in the SharePoint user interface.

Outlook Social Connector for My Sites

Although not part of My Sites, the Outlook Social Connector connects to the My Site Host to displays newsfeed items from a user's My Site when you view an email from that user. It will also update the contacts in Microsoft Outlook (you can choose whether this is done automatically or if you are prompted to accept changes). The connector can be configured so that your My Site photos display in Outlook, providing visual recognition for everyone on the email thread (provided you have a profile picture and everyone in the thread is a part of your SharePoint farm). This is a built-in feature of Outlook 2010, but a download is available from Microsoft to allow you to connect with Outlook 2007. Implementing the social connector really highlights the value of keeping the My Sites up to date. Every time you receive an email from someone, you will see his activity feed and potentially his profile picture. In my experience, the social connector has been met with great enthusiasm. If you find it distracting, you can always turn off the Social Connector in your Outlook settings.

Chapter 2
The User Profile Service

It is essential to have user profiles if you are going to have My Sites, so the first step in getting your My Site implementation going is getting the User Profile Service (UPS) up and running. The UPS in Microsoft SharePoint 2010 is much more complicated than in SharePoint 2007, but with some careful preparation, you can overcome this hurdle. One of the main reasons for the complexities is that the SharePoint 2010 UPS incorporates Forefront Identity Manager (FIM). This is not the full FIM product sold by Microsoft; rather, it's the tools representing a small subset of the FIM family. Another reason is that profiles in SharePoint 2010 can be a two-way street, with user-entered data written back to Active Directory (AD). This can enable users to maintain some of their own information that is normally kept in AD, such as home address and telephone number. There are many topics that fall under this heading, but the first step is to import the users.

Importing Profiles from Active Directory

You can import user profile information from a number of different sources. This book only covers importing users from AD, but even that can be a challenge. There are a number of steps to follow before you create the UPS. Once these preliminary steps are completed, you can provision the UPS and create the connection to AD. Finally, you perform a full import to bring in all of the specified users and the pertinent data contained in AD.

Steps to Follow Before Provisioning

Following are the steps that you need to perform before actually provisioning the UPS. Actual provisioning occurs in Central Administration when you browse to the Manage Services On This Server section, and then click Start on User Profile Synchronization. If you try to provision without paying careful attention to the following items, you might end up having to delete the User Profile Synchronization Service and start from scratch. The items to check are as follows:

1. Log on to the server on which you are going to run the User Profile Synchronization Service as the farm administrator account.

2. Ensure that both FIM services are enabled (Forefront Identity Manager Service and Forefront Identity Manager Synchronization Service) and using a domain account (as opposed to Local Service). You can locate the FIM services by going to the Services console located under Administrative Tools on the server you logged on to.

3. On the server that is going to run the User Profile Synchronization service, place the farm account in the local Administrators group. This group can be located in the Computer Management console, which you will find in Administrative Tools. This account need only be a member of the local Administrators group during provisioning. After provisioning, you should remove the farm account from this group (if you don't, a warning will appear in the Health Analyzer).

4. The synchronization account (the account that connects to AD) must have Replicate Directory Changes permission. This is not a permission normally given to accounts.

   For more information, you can refer to the TechNet article, which is available at http://technet.microsoft.com/en-us/library/ee721049.aspx#RDCconfig.

   You will need the full version of Microsoft SQL Server; the Express version will not work. If you have SQL Server 2008, you will need SP1 and CU2. I would recommend going up to the R2 version, if you can.

Steps to Follow After Provisioning

Following are the steps that you need to perform after provisioning. Be aware that it can take 10–15 minutes to provision the User Profile Synchronization Service, so you'll need to be patient.

1. After provisioning, perform an IISRESET if the server on which you are running the service is the same server that hosts Central Administration (this is true for most farms).

   On the Manage Services On Server page, you should see both the UPS and User Profile Synchronization Service started. If not, you need to start over and determine what went wrong. Usually, the problem is related to permissions.

2. Create the connection to AD. To get to the UPS page, go to Manage Service Applications, and then click the UPS that you just created.

   This is the perfect time to copy the URL and add it to the Resources on the home page of Central Administration. This will provide a shortcut to the UPS page from the home page of Central Administration, with which you can bypass this multi-stepped navigation.

3. Create the Synchronization Connection by clicking Configure Synchronization Connections in the Synchronization area, as shown here:

Synchronization
Configure Synchronization Connections | Configure Synchronization Timer Job |
Configure Synchronization Settings | Start Profile Synchronization

4. Click Create New Connection.

   You can create more than one connection if you have more than one data source, but start with one to verify that everything is working.

5. Enter the appropriate information for your AD connection.

   Ensure that the account that you are using has the appropriate permissions (for instance, Replicate Directory Changes). If the appropriate permissions are missing, it will appear as if the service is working, but the synchronization will fail. This will most likely be evidenced by the lack of connection showing up in the list after you leave the page.

6. After creating the connection, you can enter the connection filter information by clicking the connection and choosing Edit Connection Filters from the drop-down menu. On the Edit Connection Filters page, you can choose exclusion filters for groups and users. Rarely will you want to have a full import without any filters, because this will include every AD account (including test accounts and inactive accounts). These filters can be added later, but if you know the information, go ahead and include it.

7. At this point, you may create any new user profile properties and map them to their respective AD properties.

   While there are many synchronized properties included by default, there will probably be some additional ones that you want. You can always do this later, but since you are about to carry out a full synchronization, it makes sense to do it now.

8. Once the connection is configured, click Start Profile Synchronization, and then choose Start Full Synchronization. This full synchronization need only be done once, unless you add, remove, or change a user profile property that connects to AD.

9. After the synchronization is complete and you have validated that the data has been correctly imported, you can set up incremental synchronization.

   I would recommend a fairly frequent incremental update (such as once an hour), especially if the AD data changes frequently. In smaller companies, this is not as important because the changes are not as frequent.

Reprovisioning the UPS

This section is included because you might be unfortunate enough to need to reprovision the UPS. If you must do this, you run the risk of losing all the user profile information that isn't stored in AD. There is no single reason why this happens, but I have seen it occur when a cumulative update is performed. The following are the steps to carry out if you are unlucky enough to need to do this. After each Windows PowerShell command, press the Enter key and wait for the command to finish.

1. Back up the Profile Database, the Synch Database, and the Social Database. The Profile Database is the most important, but back up all of them to be sure.

2. Write down any pertinent information about the AD connection.

3. Follow the steps outlined in the section "Steps to Follow Before Provisioning," earlier in the chapter.

4. Open the SharePoint 2010 Management Shell.

5. Stop the SharePoint Timer Service by going to the Services console, or through the command line by typing **net stop sptimerv4**.

6. Find the GUID of the User Profile Sync Database in the list of database names and GUIDs returned by typing **Get-SPDatabase**.

7. Copy the GUID, and then type **$db=Get-SPDatabase –ID *<GUID>***.

8. Now that you have the database ID, unprovision it by typing the command **$db. Unprovision()**.

9. Place if offline by typing **$db.Status = 'Offline'**.

   The User Profile Synchronization Service is now unprovisioned. At this point, you need to obtain the GUID of the User Profile Service by typing **Get-SPServiceApplication**, and then look for the line with User Profile Service in it. Copy the GUID.

10. Type **$ups=GetSPServiceApplication –ID *<GUID>***.

11. Reset the synchronization by typing **$ups.ResetSynchronizationMachine()**.

12. Reset the database by typing **$ups.ResetSynchronizationDatabase()**.

13. Provision the synchronization database by typing **$db.Provision()**.

14. If the SQL Server database is on another server, ensure that the service account that the User Profile Synchronization Service runs under is the owner of the synchronization database (usually named Sync DB).

15. Restart the SharePoint Timer Service by typing **Restart-Service SPTimerV4**.

16. Start the User Profile Synchronization Service in Central Administration> Services on This Server.

    Wait for it to finish. Be sure to perform the IISRESET if Central Administration is on the same server. In fact, it won't hurt just to do it anyway.

17. Rebuild the connection string and perform a full import.

18. If for some reason the profile database (for example, Profile DB) doesn't have the old data in it, you can restore the individual database via Microsoft SQL Server, and it should retain the profile data. Use SQL Server's overwrite method to restore the backup into the existing Profile DB.

Profile Pictures

One of the key profile properties is the *Picture* property. This property allows SharePoint to display an image of the user in various places throughout SharePoint. The most obvious of those is the picture shown on the profile.aspx page. Once the user (or UPS administrator) has uploaded a profile picture, it is available not only throughout the SharePoint farm, but by any program that has the ability to connect to the SharePoint farm and use its web services. A quality profile picture is one of the most effective ways to increase My Site usage. Profile pictures should be square, properly lit, and a good representation of the person. It doesn't need to be a glamour shot, but is should be tastefully done. The separation of social networks for work and personal life often blur, but it is important to try to keep them apart. A business-appropriate profile picture can help to maintain this separation.

Profile Picture Storage

In SharePoint 2007, profile pictures were normally stored in the personal sites of each user without any parsing. When the profile picture was pulled up on a webpage, it had to be sized. In SharePoint 2010, a profile picture is converted into three different thumbnails, but the original file is not stored, so users can upload large images without filling up the content database or taking up personal site quota space. The total amount of space required for all three thumbnails runs about 40 kb at the most, per person. The thumbnails are stored in the following location in the My Site Host:

```
http://<my site host>/user photos/profile pictures
```

The three thumbnail sizes are 144 x 144, 96 x 96, and 32 x 32, and the file names are based upon the domain name (if the users are based on AD). The following list shows the formulas for the file names:

Large (144 x 144)	domain_ntlogin_LThumb
Medium (96 x 96)	domain_ntlogin_MThumb
Small (32 x 32)	domain_ntlogin_SThumb

Upgrading from SharePoint 2007

If you are upgrading your My Site Host from SharePoint 2007 as part of an in-place upgrade from SharePoint Server 2007 to 2010, the profile pictures are not automatically changed into thumbnails; they are simply left in the same location. Luckily, there is a PowerShell command that converts the pictures into thumbnails (and thereby increasing the performance of the My Site Host). The command is as follows:

```
Update-SPProfilePhotoStore
```

The command won't work if you manually put the profile picture locations into a brand new My Site Host. It must be an in-place upgrade.

Chapter 3
Setting Up My Sites

Setting up a My Site Host is an important step that commands a certain amount of thinking before you start. The first thing you want to consider is whether it will be in its own web application or part of another one. Proper consideration will save you a lot of trouble down the road. Since the My Site Host is going to be a separate site collection anyway, it is almost always best to create it in its own web application. That way, if there are issues with wayward code in an individual's My Site, it won't bring down your intranet (or extranet) and vice versa. Also, keeping the My Site Host in its own content database is a good decision, especially if you are going to have personal site collections. This keeps your main (non-My Site) content database more trim and easier to maintain and back up.

The second item that you want to consider is what to name the My Site. You might be thinking right now that you can always change it if you want. Although this might be technically true, it can cause problems later on. If you change the URL of your My Site Host after users have connected to it with Microsoft Outlook in any fashion, these users will be repeatedly prompted to log on at random times. This is because Outlook is trying to synchronize data to a location that no longer exists. Also, if you are using the My Site Outlook Social Connector, the connector will need to be reconfigured by each individual. There are lots of popular options for My Site Host names; Home, My, and MySite are the most common ones I have come across. I recommend making the My Site name something that is easy to spell and makes sense to the people who are going to use it. If you are going to deploy My Sites in multiple countries or with multiple languages, it might make more sense to either use a host name that works with all groups, or to have a different My Site Host for each of the distinctive groups.

The third point of consideration is how many My Site Hosts you want to create. Using multiple My Site Hosts makes sense if you have sets of users with distinctively different needs. These user sets can be distinguished by employment status, such as whether they are contractors or regular employees. There might also be a separation that is security based such as the clear-ance level of an employee. There is also the concern about language differences. It's much easier to create different My Site Hosts than to create variations on a single one. Among the reasons for this is that the My Site Host has several pages (even though it looks like one) and you might want to send the employee or user to a particular site no matter what the browser setting says.

Although the choices involved in provisioning the My Site Host can be intimidating, as long as you plan ahead, you should be okay when creating it, so don't worry too much about messing it up. You can always start with a pilot group and see how your initial settings work out before committing to any particular scenario. In the worst case, you can change it. The personal sites can be backed up and moved without too much difficulty, and the Microsoft SharePoint User Profile Service (UPS) stores the users' data independent of the My Site Host, so you don't need to worry about losing profile information the users have entered.

Quotas

There is a lot to consider when you set up quotas for personal site collections. The My Site Host doesn't need to have a quota set on it because there should be only a few people with rights to add content to it. A large part of the determination of these quotas is to determine how you want users to treat My Sites. If you are going to remove file share access from users (such as removing a "home" drive) for personal storage, you will want to provide a larger storage area. In my experience, most people won't come close to consuming a reasonably sized quota, but some people will quickly fill it up. An administrator must also consider that some people will want to treat My Site as their personal storage of media files, which is fine if you plan for it, but this can quickly fill up your database if you don't. Here are some general rules of thumb to follow:

- Keep each content database below 200 GB. This is for performance and disaster recovery concerns. So, if you allow 5 GB per person, you will need a content database for every 40 people (60 if you don't expect people to fill them up). Note that 5 GB might be unrealistic in organizations with lots of users.

- Files are blocked at a web application level, so if you only have one My Site Host, everyone will have the same set of blocked files. Consider blocking media types if you don't want people uploading their music files and videos. Most executable type files (for example, .exe, .com, .vbs, .js, and so on) are blocked by default, but it doesn't hurt to review the list as technology changes.

- All items in the site collection plus any subsites count against the quota. Also, any items in the top-level Recycle Bin count against it. If versioning is turned on, then those versions count against it, as well. Potentially, a user could have very few visible (or zero) items and still run out of quota space.

Setting Personal Site Quotas

My Site quotas are managed in the same place as other quotas by going to Central Administration, clicking Application Management, and then choosing Configure Quotas And Locks. Here, you can specify which site collections use which quota templates, and give individuals their own quotas, depending on individual needs. By default, personal sites are given the quota template named Personal Site. To modify this quota template, go to Specify Quota Templates (note that if you have not yet created a My Site host but would like to plan ahead, you can go ahead and create a new quota and name it whatever you want). You will want to choose the Personal Site to modify as shown in the following screenshot. The screenshot shows that this quota has a limit of only 100 MB—hardly any space at all these days. So, modifying early on is definitely a good thing if you actually want people to use their personal sites for documents and you have the capacity in your database.

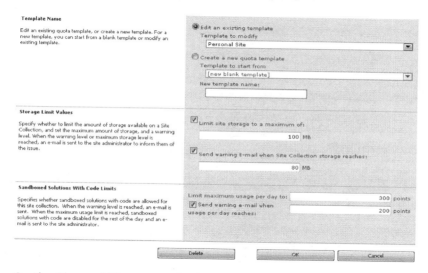

On the Personal Site quota template page, you can change the items as you see fit, including setting limits on the sandboxed solutions. This can be important if you are running into performance issues, but it only affects those solutions that are deployed to places that use this template (for instance, personal sites). You might think you are done once you have modified the template, but sites don't automatically update with the new template. You can apply the new quota to each site collection on the Central Administration page by clicking Application Management | Configure Quotas And Locks (which could take hours if you have a lot of personal sites already in place), or you can use PowerShell to apply the modified template to all existing sites in a single update. Use the cmdlet *Set-SPSite* in conjunction with *Get-SPSite* to avoid having to run the command for each personal site collection. The command is shown in the following:

```
Get-SPSite -Limit ALL -WebApplication $MySiteHost |%{  Set-SPSite -QuotaTemplate "Personal
Site" -Identity $_.Url }
```

Replace $MySiteHost with your My Site host URL (for example, http://mysite/) without the path name ("personal"). This command will also set the quota of the My Site host. If needed, the My Site Host quota can then be modified to different settings; doing so affects new My Sites created from the host but does not affect existing ones. Also, if you decided to make a new quota template, replace "Personal Site" in the command with the appropriate template name. Finally, if users have individual quotas, these are overwritten and need to be reapplied. Since this is normally the exception and not the rule, this bulk update should still save you a lot of time.

Visual Upgrade on Site Collections

If you are upgrading from SharePoint 2007, there is an issue to cover with regard to setting up the My Site Host. The existing My Sites will retain the 2007 look and feel, so you will need to do a visual upgrade on the site collections at some point. You can do this from PowerShell by using the following bit of code:

```
$site=Get-SPWeb <URL of Site>
$site.VisualUpgradeWebs()
```

Replace <URL of Site> with the URL of the site that you want to upgrade. Of course, you probably don't want to do this on a site-by-site basis, so once you have tested a few site collections (and the top-level site collection), you can use some piping to get the command to run on all the site collections at once. You can do this by using the following PowerShell code:

```
$web = Get-SPWebApplication <URL of My Site Host> |
foreach{$site in $web.sites){$site.VisualUpgradeWebs()}
```

If you need to go back to the 2007 version (known as version 3), you can run the following PowerShell code:

```
Get-SPSite <URL of My Site Host> |
Foreach{$_.UIVersionConfigurationEnabled=1;$_.UIVersion=3;$_.Update();
```

You will need to put in the URL of your My Site host. This changes everything back to the SharePoint 2007 version including the My Site host. You should only do this if for some reason something doesn't work (for example, a SharePoint 2007–specific Web Part).

Chapter 4
Multiple Farms and My Sites

The addition of service applications has produced many benefits to Microsoft SharePoint 2010, but it has also created some challenges. The major benefit is that one farm can consume (use) another farm's User Profile Service (UPS). This keeps all the user profile information synchronized without the need for replication. Replication is still a valid option for keeping user profile data in synchronized among various farms. The difference is in control. If you want centralized control of all the user data, then consuming the UPS is the proper method to choose.

Connecting to Another Farm's User Profile Service

Before any farm can provide services to another farm, the consuming farm must be able to use the Application Discovery and Load Balancer Service, also known as the Topology Service. Once that has been done, then other services can be published and consumed. The process to connect two farms requires many steps and care must be taken to perform them correctly. The major steps are separated below. Be sure to complete each one before moving on to the next step.

Step 1: Set Up the Application Discovery and Load Balancer Service Application

The part we are concerned with here is that of Application Discovery. The consumer needs rights to use the service so that it can find the proxies on the publishing farm. To do this, follow these steps:

On the Consumer Farm

1. Open the SharePoint 2010 Management Shell using an account with SP-ShellAdmin rights.

2. Type **(Get-SPFarm).Id**, and then press Enter.

3. Copy the output to Notepad (or just keep Notepad open so you can type it in).

On the Publishing Farm

1. Open the SharePoint 2010 Management Shell using an account with SP-ShellAdmin rights.

2. Type **$security = Get-SPTopologyServiceApplication | Get-SPServiceApplicationSecurity**, and then press Enter.

3. Type **$claimProvider = (Get-SPClaimProvider System).ClaimProvider**, and then press Enter.

4. Type **$principal = New-SPClaimsPrincipal –ClaimType "http://schemas.micro-soft.com/sharepoint/2009/08/claims/farmid" -ClaimProvider $claimProvider -ClaimValue *<paste the farm id from step 1 here just as it appeared>***, and then press Enter.

5. Type **Grant-SPObjectSecurity -Identity $security -Principal $principal -Rights "Full Control"**, and then press Enter.

6. Type **Get-SPTopologyServiceApplication | Set-SPServiceApplicationSecurity -ObjectSecurity $security**, and then press Enter.

Step 2: Create the Certificates

To establish a trusted relationship between farms, you need to exchange certificates between servers. The consumer will need the root certificate of the publishing farm, and the publishing farm will need both the root certificate of the consumer and the Security Token Service (STS) certificate. For more information about how to do this, read the TechNet article at *http://technet.microsoft.com/en-us/library/ee704552.aspx*, or perform the following steps.

On the Consumer Farm

1. Open the SharePoint 2010 Management Shell.

2. Type **$rootCert = (Get-SPCertificateAuthority).RootCertificate**, and then press Enter.

3. Type **$rootCert.Export("Cert") | Set-Content C:\ConsumingFarmRoot.cer -Encoding byte**, and then press Enter (you can choose a different location/filename if you want).

   You now have the root certificate for the consuming server on its C drive. Next, you get the STS certificate.

4. Type **$stsCert = (Get-SPSecurityTokenServiceConfig).LocalLoginProvider. SigningCertificate**, and then press Enter.

5. Type **$stsCert.Export("Cert") | Set-Content C:\ConsumingFarmSTS.cer -Encoding byte**, and then press Enter.

   You now have the STS token for the consuming farm.

   Make the two files you created available to the publishing farm (copy them to the publishing farm)

On the Publishing Farm

1. Open the SharePoint 2010 Management Shell.

2. Type **$rootCert = (Get-SPCertificateAuthority).RootCertificate**, and then press Enter.

3. Type **$rootCert.Export("Cert") | Set-Content C:\PublishingFarmRoot.cer -Encoding byte**, and then press Enter.

   Make the file available on the consuming farm.

Step 3: Import the Certificates

The publishing server must trust the consuming server before it will send content to it. You do this by setting up trust through certificates. The publishing server needs the certificate created in Step 2. To import the consumer root certificates on the publishing server, perform the following steps:

1. Open the SharePoint 2010 Management Shell on the publishing server.

2. Type **$stsCert = Get-PfxCertificate *C:\ConsumingFarmRoot.cer***, and then press Enter (replace *C:\ConsumingFarmRoot.cer* with the location of the consuming farm root cert, if you saved it to a different location).

3. Type **New-SPTrustedRootAuthority <name of the consuming server> -Certificate $trustCert**, and then press Enter.

   The certificate should print to the screen, if it was successful.

To import the consumer STS certificate on the publishing server, follow these steps:

1. Open the SharePoint 2010 Management Shell on the publishing server.

2. Type **$stsCert = Get-PfxCertificate *C:\ConsumingFarmSTS.cer,*** and then press Enter (replace *C:\ConsumingFarmSTS.cer* with location of consuming server STS certificate).

3. Type **New-SPTrustedServiceTokenIssuer *<name of consuming server>* -Certificate $stsCert**, and press Enter.

   The certificate should print to the screen, if it was successful.

To import the publishing root certificate on the consuming server, perform the following steps:

1. Open the SharePoint 2010 Management Shell on the consuming server.

2. Type **$trustCert = Get-PfxCertificate *C:\PublishingFarmRoot.cer***, and then press Enter (replace *C:\PublishingFarmRoot.cer* with the location of the publishing farm root certificate).

3. Type **New-SPTrustedRootAuthority *<name of the publishing server>* -Certificate $trustCert**, and then press Enter.

   The certificate should print to the screen, if it was successful.

Step 4: Publish the Service

You must publish the service from the publishing server before it can be consumed. Publishing a service acknowledges the intent to share and makes the service available for discovery by consuming farms. The easiest way to do this is from Central Administration, following these steps:

1. Browse to the Central Administration site of the publishing server.

2. Click Manage Service Applications.

3. Click to select the UPS (click just to the right of the service name. You don't want to manage it, just highlight it).

4. Click the Publish icon at the top of the page.

5. Verify that the Publish This Service Application To Other Farms check box is selected.

6. Copy the Published URL. This is a very long string that looks similar to the following:

   ```
   urn:schemas-microsoft-com:sharepoint:service:6f63cdec5e784a02b2b79f9bf91346af#authorit
   y=urn:uuid:daf0ec20a27a44c7abe5104b5d516637&authority=https://myserver:1111/Topology/
   topology.svc
   ```

7. Click OK. You're done with the publishing server.

Step 5: Consume the Service

1. Open the Central Administration of the consuming server.

2. Click Manage Service Applications.

3. On the top ribbon, click the Connect icon, and then choose User Profile Service Application Proxy.

4. In the Connect To A Remote Service Application dialog box, paste the URL from the Published URL (your actual URL, not the one from the example).

5. Click OK. You should see a screen similar to the following (or an error page if it couldn't connect).

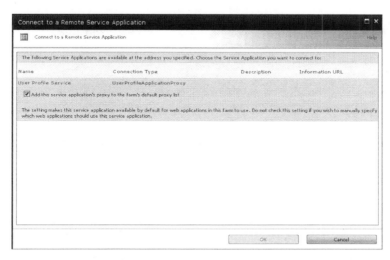

6. Highlight User Profile Service, and then click OK.

7. Accept the default name for the connection or modify it to reflect the source server name. Leave the Add This Service Application's Proxy To The Farm's Default Proxy List check box selected. This will make all new web application default to the consumed service. Click OK.

8. A confirmation screen appears. Click OK.

You have now consumed the UPS. That means when a user updates their profile data, it will be the same on both farms. It will use the trusted My Site locations, the audiences, and so on from the publishing farm. Therefore, if you want to add or modify anything for the consumer farm, the change must be made on the Central Administration of the publishing farm.

User Profile Replication

User profile replication is different from consuming another farm's UPS. The main difference is that replication actually moves a copy of the data from one farm to another. This is most useful for scenarios in which you want to locate My Site Hosts in different areas geographically or logistically, but you want the user data to be the same in each location. For example, suppose that your company has two locations that are distant from one another such as Iceland and Australia. For reasons such as bandwidth and latency, you want people in each location to have their personal My Site located near them. With user profile replication, you can keep all the employee profile data current in both location and provide localized searching of user profile data. Another reason for replicating data could be to keep different versions of SharePoint in synchronization, which offers the added benefit of a more graceful migration strategy.

The User Profile Replication Engine

The User Profile Replication Engine can be found in the SharePoint 2010 Administration Toolkit. The Toolkit is available as a free download from Microsoft. Once you install the replication engine, its icon appears on the desktop. You should install the Toolkit on the server where the receiving UPS resides. The replication engine is composed of two parts:

- Windows Service
- Windows PowerShell snap-ins

The Windows Service should not be stopped or started by using the Services MMC; rather, you should use the newly added PowerShell cmdlets. The cmdlets are accessed by clicking the replication engine icon on the desktop of the server. To start and configure the replication, log on to the server where the replication engine is installed using an account that has Manage Profiles permissions (additionally Manage Social data, if you plan to replicate tags and notes, too) access to the UPS on all the servers involved in the replication. See the following TechNet Article reference for the permission and patch level requirements for replication between farms. The cmdlet-centric user interface in the 2010 version is a departure from the graphical user interface used with the SharePoint 2007 Administration Toolkit, and it is a bit more cumbersome to use. It requires some basic knowledge of PowerShell, but you should be able to get it going without too many problems. Be sure to document the settings if you use any of the optional parameters.

A TechNet article about the User Profile Replication Engine can be found at http://technet. microsoft.com/en-us/library/cc663011.aspx, and you can download the SharePoint Administrator's Toolkit with the Replication Engine from http://go.microsoft.com/ fwlink/?LinkId=196866.

When you plan your ongoing replication scenario, you will want to think of it as pushing data. This will simplify your replication scenario. The exception is when you are setting up replication for the first time. For the initial replication, you want to pull a single "gold" set of user profile information from an up-to-date source. In subsequent replications, you should push the incremental profile data changes from the site that houses that particular group's My Sites. For example, if you have three regions—Asia, North America, and Europe—changes made to a European user's My Site will be pushed to Asia and North America. This scenario ensures that every farm has a current User Profile database.

The *Get-SPProfilePropertyCollection* Cmdlet

This cmdlet will bring back all the properties from the User Profile Service that is associated with the My Site Host identified by the *Source* variable. The output is an Enter-delimited list that can be piped to a file or to another PowerShell cmdlet.

Usage

```
Get-SPProfilePropertyCollection [-Source] <String>
```

Argument Definitions		
Source	Required	Specifies the URL of the My Site host.

The *Start-SPProfileServiceFullReplication* Cmdlet

You will probably only run this cmdlet once, when you want to transfer all the user profile data from a source server and before you start incremental replication. The incremental replication can only go back 14 days, so you will need to run this if you want a full set of user profile data. You can run this cmdlet without the need to set up credentials and you should run it on the server that is receiving the user profile data.

You should disable Simple Mail Transfer Protocol (SMTP) on the receiving farm before performing a full replication. Otherwise, the profile update will be seen as new information, and email will be sent to users regarding their "new" colleagues. Disable SMTP by removing the outgoing server name in Central Administration | System Settings | Configure Outgoing E-mail Settings. Re-enter the mail server name after replication is complete.

Usage

Pipe the results of *Get-SPProfilePropertyCollection* into this cmdlet.

```
Start-SPProfileServiceFullReplication -Destination <String> -Source <String>
[-ActiveDirectoryDomains <String[]>] [-DoSocialReplication <SwitchParameter>]
[-DoUpgrade <SwitchParameter>] [-EnableInstrumentation <SwitchParameter>] [-MatchSubtype
<SwitchParameter>] [-MaxNumberOfThreads <Int32>] [-NumberOfRetry <Int32>] [-Properties
<String[]>] [-StartAtIndex <Int32>] [-Timeout <Int32>]
```

Argument Definitions		
Destination	Required	The URL of the destination My Site Host.
Source	Required	The URL of the source My Site Host.
ActiveDirectoryDomains	Optional	The domains of the Active Directories that you want replicated. The default is all.
DoSocialReplication	Optional	Replicates social tags, notes, and ratings. Not valid for SharePoint 2007.
DoUpgrade	Optional	Must be used if source is a SharePoint 2007 server and destination is a 2010 SharePoint server

Argument Definitions		
EnableInstrumentation	Optional	Logs detailed data in instrumentation log.
MatchSubType	Optional	Helps prevent mismatches before source and destination.
MaxNumberOfThreads	Optional	Use to throttle down resources used. Default is 25.
NumberOfRetry	Optional	Specifies how many times to try in case of a failure. The default is 10.
Properties	Optional	Properties to replicate. The default is all.
StartAtIndex	Optional	Specifies which profile index to start at. The default is zero.
Timeout	Optional	Specifies the time to wait before timing out.

The *Start-SPProfileServiceIncrementalReplication* Cmdlet

This cmdlet will replicate any changes to the user profile information, including properties, social tags, notes, and ratings. Information that is controlled by Active Directory is not replicated. The replication engine uses the audiences and trusted My Site locations to determine what user data needs to be replicated.

> **Note** Verify that the trusted My Site locations have been properly configured before you run this.

Before you run this, you will need to set the credentials. This process specifies the user name and password under which to perform the replication. This can be done in one of two ways. Using the first method, in Administrative Tools, go to the Services console, click Replication Engine, and then set the permissions there. With the second method, you can use the *Get-Credential* cmdlet to set the credentials and then pass those credentials as a property. If you want to add a destination for the replication, you must stop the Replication Engine Service by using *Stop-SPProfileServiceIncrementalReplication*, and then use this command to start it again, providing the destinations. The easiest way to do this is to restart the incremental profile replication without the *Destination* parameter; you will be prompted to enter the destinations one after the other until you are done (at which time you just press Enter). You will need to do this every time you want to add or remove a destination.

Usage

Pipe the results of *Get-SPProfilePropertyCollection* into this cmdlet.

```
Start-SPProfileServiceIncrementalReplication -Destination <String[]> -Source <String>
[-ActiveDirectoryDomains <String[]>] [-Credential <PSCredential>] [-DoSocialReplication
<SwitchParameter>] [-DoUpgrade <SwitchParameter>] [-EnableInstrumentation <SwitchParameter>]
[-FeedProperties <String[]>] [-MatchSubtype <SwitchParameter>] [-NumberOfRetry
<Int32>] [-Properties <String[]>] [-ReplicationInterval <Int32>] [-Timeout <Int32>]
[-WaitTimeBetweenFailures <Int32>]
```

Argument Definitions

Destination	Required	The URL of the destination My Site Host.
Source	Required	The URL of the source My Site Host.
ActiveDirectoryDomains	Optional	The domains of the Active Directories that you want replicated. The default is all.
Credential	Optional	Specifies the credentials with which to run the replication.
DoSocialReplication	Optional	Enables the replication of social tags, notes, and ratings.
DoUpgrade	Optional	Must be used if source is a SharePoint 2007 server and destination is 2010.
EnableInstrumentation	Optional	Enables detailed logging to the instrumentation log.
FeedProperties	Optional	Ignore trusted My Site Host locations.
MatchSubType	Optional	Helps to prevent mismatches before source and destination.
NumberOfRetry	Optional	Specifies how many times to try in case of a failure. The default is 10.
Properties	Optional	Properties to replicate. The default is all.
Timeout	Optional	Specifies the time to wait before timing out.
WaitTimeBetweenFailures	Optional	Amount of time in seconds that the User Profile Replication Engine should wait after a failure before trying again. The default is 300 (5 minutes).

Example

```
$myCredentials = Get-Crendential
Start-SPProfileServiceIncrementalReplication -Destination http://server1/my -Source http://
server2/my -Credential $myCredentials
```

Note If you get a permissions error and you know that the permissions are correct, try using the server name and port number instead of the friendly URL. The Alternate Access Mappings might not be properly set with the correct defaults. In any case, the server name and port number should work.

The *Stop-SPProfileServiceIncrementalReplication* Cmdlet

This cmdlet stops User Profile Service Replication Engine Windows Service. It should always be used instead of manually stopping the service via the MMC service console. Use it to stop incremental replication on the source server. This cmdlet takes no arguments.

Usage

```
Stop-SPProfileServiceIncrementalReplication
```

Using Managed Metadata from Another Farm

Keeping managed metadata pruned and useful is hard enough in one farm, much less having to do it in multiple farms. Ideally, you want to have one managed metadata center and have all the farms consume it. This can be done in the same way as consuming the UPS. There is one restriction to consuming the Managed Metadata Service (MMS): if the consuming farm has its own My Site Host, it must also have its own MMS. The consuming farm may, however, have two Managed Metadata Service Applications: one that connects to the publishing farm, and one that exists only on the consuming farm. If you want users to have personal My Site collections on the consuming farm, you cannot consume the UPS, as well. If you don't need personal My Site collections on the consuming farm, then you can consume both the managed metadata and the UPS applications.

Using Another Farm's Managed Metadata in Profile Properties

Follow the steps shown earlier in this chapter to connect to a UPS, changing the references from "User Profile Service" to "Managed Metadata Service." If you have already done the Application Discovery, Load Balancer Service Application, and the certificates, you won't need to perform those steps.

1. On the publishing farm, browse to the Manage Service Applications page from Central Administration.

2. Highlight the Managed Metadata Service, and then click the Publish icon.

3. Copy the Published URL and put it someplace convenient such as Notepad.

4. On the consuming farm, browse to the Manage Service Applications page from Central Administration.

5. Click Connect, and then choose Managed Metadata Service Connection.

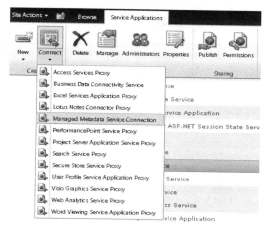

6. In the Connect To A Remote Service Application dialog box, paste the Published URL from step 3, and then click OK.

7. Highlight the line that begins with Managed Metadata Service, and then click OK.

8. On the confirmation page, click OK again. You should now be connected.

   You now need to create a normal Managed Metadata Service on the consuming farm. When you create the new Managed Metadata Service, it should be the default.

Also, ensure that the Managed Metadata Web Service is running in Manage Services On Server in Central Administration, as shown in the following:

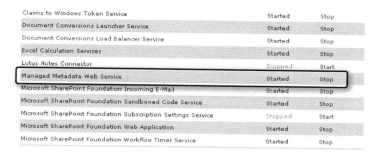

You should be able to tie the published term store to the user profile properties on the consuming server by choosing the appropriate term store categories. These categories will be available if you have successfully connected to the MMS on the publishing farm.

Chapter 5
Customizing My Site Navigation

There are two levels of navigation in My Sites: a top level of navigation and a sub level which forms the tabs. The top level of navigation is a conglomeration of three different sources: the top level of the My Site Host, the top navigation items of the My Site Host, and the set of personalization sites that fall within the audiences of the user. The top navigation items of the My Site Host can be modified by clicking the Top Link Bar link under Site Settings. The tabs are in the middle of the screen on the default pages, and they are controlled by the Quick Launch settings under Site Settings. If you want to add or remove tabs, you can do so under that section. Keep in mind that if you add any new tabs, you will need to do the styling yourself. Each tab is an individual page and must be modified as such. There are some other navigation elements in the My Site Host. There is the Welcome button, the View My Profile As Seen By, and the Site Actions button. Clearly, there are a lot of navigation elements to consider, and modifying them should be done with a keen eye to usability. Making My Sites more confusing will do no one any good.

Modifying the Top-Level Navigation

There are a couple of ways to modify the top-level navigation item out of the box. The easiest is to go to Site Actions | Site Settings, and then click the Top Link Bar link under the Look and Feel heading, as shown in the following:

If you modify the My Site Host Top Link bar, it will affect all sites contained within the My Site Host (unless the master page has been modified to provide custom navigation). Note that if you turn on the Publishing feature, the Top Link Bar link will disappear. You can still modify the items, but you will have to type in the link. There is another way to modify both the top-level navigation and the tabs. You can simply append **_layouts/AreaNavigationSettings. aspx** to the URL of your My Site Host to view a page where you can edit the links of both areas. The Global Navigation corresponds to the top-level navigation items between the My Site link and the personalization site links. The Current Navigation corresponds to the tabs in the middle of the pages. When you load the page, the navigation items should appear similar to the following figure:

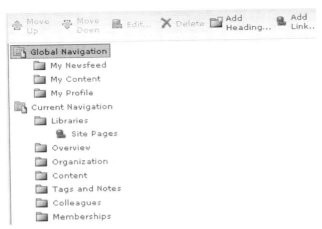

It is also much easier to modify the items by using this interface. For example, if you want to change the order of items, you can just move them up or down rather than having to reorder all the items to just swap two of them. Another reason you might want to use this page is if you are going to modify the master page to allow drop-down lists on your menu. This page is the only way to modify those menu items. You can't use the Top Link Bar to manage them. This will be very useful if you are trying to keep your navigation consistent across multiple site collections. This page doesn't let you use another site collection's navigation (that would be nice, wouldn't it?), but it will give you the tools necessary to make the changes consistent in each site collection.

Implementing Drop-Down Menus

As just mentioned, it is possible to have drop-down menus (and even fly-outs) in your top-level navigation menu. One of the main reasons to implement this is if you are trying to keep your navigation consistent across multiple site collections. This is a common goal and makes good sense from a user interface perspective. Users don't have to wonder what is in the navigation from place to place. There are a couple of things you need to do in order to make this happen. The first is that you will need to put in some drop-down navigation items. For example, the out-of-the-box navigation uses My Newsfeed as a link in the top menu bar, and it appears as a heading in the Global Navigation Editing and Sorting Section. Once you start using the drop-downs, use the Add Link option to add additional links under the headings; these are the links that will appear in the drop-down. The second thing is to modify the master page of the My Site Host. This is a little more complicated but nothing too hard. To make this happen follow these steps.

1. Open the My Site Host in SharePoint Designer.

2. Click the Master Pages item in the Navigation pane.

3. Open up the master page (verify that you have a backup of it first), which is mysite. master if you haven't changed it.

   You will need to ensure it is checked out to make changes.

4. Open the v4.master in SharePoint Designer, and then copy the SharePoint:AspMenu tag that has the ID of TopNavigationMenuV4.

5. Paste the tag into the mysite.master within the tags to start and end the "PlaceHolderHorizontalNav" Content Placeholder.

6. Ensure that the StaticDisplayLevels is set to 2 and MaximumDynamicDisplayLevels is set to 1 so that it appears as follows (these are the defaults in v4.master):

```
<SharePoint:AspMenu
  ID="TopNavigationMenuV4"
  Runat="server"
  EnableViewState="false"
  DataSourceID="topSiteMap"
  AccessKey="<%$Resources:wss,navigation_accesskey%>"
  UseSimpleRendering="true"
  UseSeparateCss="false"
  Orientation="Horizontal"
  StaticDisplayLevels="2"
  MaximumDynamicDisplayLevels="1"
  SkipLinkText=""
  Visible="false"
  CssClass="s4-tn"/>
```

7. Save the mysite.master page and check in a major version.

The menu should have drop-down items now. If you don't apply the new master page to the system pages it might look strange, but because only a few people should ever see that page, it isn't as big a problem. This is due to the large number of items that will appear in the Top Link Bar. To avoid this, simply make your modified master page the same for both types of pages. Personalization sites will continue to show the old menu style unless a modified master page is applied to them, as well. The master page changes in the My Site Host do not filter down.

Modifying the Tab Section

The Tab section—or as I like to refer to it, the sub navigation—is controlled by the Quick Launch under Site Actions | Site Settings. Each tab represents a different page. It's easy to delete pages but a lot harder to add them. If you are going to add a new tab, you should copy one of the first three pages (something like Organization, which has less to remove, would be a good choice) and remove the content below the tab bar. This will ensure that the top part remains consistent. Of course, if you don't want the top part to remain consistent, you still want to start with a copy of one of the pages so that you maintain the content areas and My Site specific code. The Quick Launch is used the same way as other sites, as shown here:

The interface is pretty straightforward, but it is also fairly simple. You won't be changing it much, so it isn't too much of an issue.

Modifying View My Profile As Seen By

If company policy states that all profile properties seen on the Overview page (person.aspx) should be visible to everyone (in your organization), you can get back the space used by this control and make the page look cleaner. This comes under my philosophy of making things simpler, if possible. There are some obvious reasons to keep the control visible such as controlling who can see mobile numbers. If you decide to not show the control, it is recommended that you don't remove web controls, in case other Web Parts reference them, and removing controls might cause problems when performing upgrades to future versions of SharePoint. If you want to get the space back, open person.aspx in SharePoint Designer (using Edit File in Advanced Mode), and then go to the code window. Look for this line of code:

```
<SPSWC:AsSeenBy runat="server" id="ddlAsSeenBy" SelectionMode="Single" autopostback="true"/>
```

Add **Visible="false"** so that it looks like the following code:

```
<SPSWC:AsSeenBy runat="server" id="ddlAsSeenBy" SelectionMode="Single" Visible="false"
autopostback="true"/>
```

The control defaults to Everyone, so the user's profile will look the same to themselves as it does to everyone else.

Adding Personalization Sites

Personalization sites are one of the most underutilized yet most beneficial parts of the My Site experience. They were created so that sites could be targeted to groups of users defined by audiences. When you create a Personalization site and connect it to the My Site Host, a link appears in the top navigation bar, but only to those people that are members of its target audiences. There are several examples of how this can be useful in targeting content to groups of users and encouraging users to take advantage of their My Sites more often. Here are some examples.

- Office location-specific pages
- Human Resources for different countries (or different groups of users)
- Manager-only pages
- New employee training
- Contractor page

Personalization sites can be in any site collection but appear as though they are part of the My Site Host. To create one, click Create Site, and then select the Personalization Site template. The template should appear in the list of normal site templates as shown in the following figure:

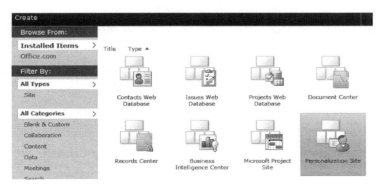

Once you have created your Personalization site and modified it the way you want, you must configure the My Site Host to display the link. To add a site, follow these steps:

1. Create audiences for the Personalization site, if they don't exist. (If the site is for all users, you can skip this step.)

2. Make sure audiences are compiled if you have created any.

   3. Go to Central Administration, and then click Service Applications | User Profile Service |
      My Site Settings | Configure Personalization Sites.

   4. Click New Item.

   5. Type the link to the Personalization site.

   6. Choose the appropriate audience or audiences, and then click Save and exit.

You should test the Personalization site with the appropriate audiences to ensure that it is
operating correctly.

> **Note** Audiences are not security groups. Just because a site link doesn't appear on a user's My
> Site doesn't mean she can't navigate to it in another manner. If you want to secure the site, you
> must use security groups and site permissions, just as you would a normal site.

Chapter 6
Modifying the My Site Host

Modifying the My Site Host can be a daunting task. It is not like other sites that can be simply modified by adding or removing Web Parts via the web user interface or by using Microsoft SharePoint Designer. Even though there are some parts of the My Site Host that can be modified in this manner, many parts cannot, so keeping all the My Site parts looking consistent requires some work. I am not trying to scare you away, but I want you to realize that this is not a quick and easy task (of course, some people think SharePoint branding is easy). So if you want to do any branding beyond Themes, just be patient and your efforts will be rewarded. This section intends to demystify the My Site Host and lets you dig in and make it work for your organization.

File Locations

There are two locations for the set of default files that are a part of the My Site Host. The first set of pages is part of the particular instance of the My Site Host; the other set is in the SharePoint hive (Program Files\Common File\Microsoft Shared\Web Server Extensions\14) on the hard disk in the _LAYOUTS directory. So, when you back up the My Site Host (by using *stsadm*, for example) the files in the _LAYOUTS directory are not part of that backup. This can cause problems if you want to customize two different My Site Hosts on the same farm, because every My Site Host uses the same files in the hive (at least by default). This is because every site in SharePoint maps virtually to the same _LAYOUTS directory. There are ways to work around this, but first let's look at the two locations and the files that are in them.

Files Accessible in SharePoint Designer

These are files that appear when you open the My Site Host URL in SharePoint Designer. You can edit them just as you would for a normal site. Most of the editable items are web controls, but generally, the items in the bottom can be edited as normal Web Parts. If you want to be able to add Web Parts on your page, you will need to add a Web Part zone, if there isn't one already. Note that if you change the top part of a page, those changes don't translate to other pages, so if you want to keep the top consistent, then you will need to make those same changes on every page. The files you can modify with SharePoint Designer are as follows.

- **Overview** (default)   person.aspx
- **Organization**   Organizationview.aspx
- **Content**   personcontent.aspx

Files in the _LAYOUTS Directory

It is much more difficult to edit files in the _LAYOUTS directory. If you want to modify these files, you need to make backups of the files and keep them in the _LAYOUTS directory. I recommend working on a copy of the file and leaving the original alone. This is because when you upgrade or apply a Service Pack, it is possible that the file will be overwritten. It is also possible that the upgrade or Service Pack might fail because the installation package is looking for specific versions of files. The _LAYOUTS directory is subject to changes, and any file you modify there should be backed up in another place. To edit these files, you need to use something other than SharePoint Designer. This can be Notepad or Microsoft Visual Studio, if it is installed on the server. The following is a list of files in the _LAYOUTS directory:

- **Document**   viewlsts.aspx
- **Tags and Notes**   thoughts.aspx
- **Colleagues**   MyContactLinks.aspx
- **Memberships**   MyMemberships.aspx

Displaying Profile Properties

One of the main reasons for having profile properties is to make relevant information about you easily accessible. Several of the out-of-the-box properties are prominently displayed, such as About Me, but in many cases, you will want to move, remove, and/or add properties. This is especially true for custom properties that have been added. Of course, you can choose to display them in the drop-down on the Overview page, but that is fairly limited, especially if you are displaying a large amount of text. Luckily, it is fairly easy to display properties wherever you want them on a page. This goes for whatever SharePoint page you are working on, even if it is outside the My Site Host.

Obtaining a User's Profile Properties

Before you can display a person's profile properties, you must obtain them from SharePoint. This can be done by using the *SPSWC:ProfilePropertyLoader* control, as shown in the following:

```
<SPSWC:ProfilePropertyLoader id="m_objLoader" LoadFullProfileOfCurrentUser="true"
runat="server"/>
```

The values are pulled by using the account name of the query string variable *accountname*. If an *accountname* is not provided, the control defaults to the current user. Place the control above any of the other controls that use any of the user profile properties so that the data will be loaded first and available to be displayed in the other controls. By default, all of the pages that come with a My Site Host will have a *SPSWC:ProfilePropertyLoader* control, but if you want to create a new page or put profile data on another page, you will need to add this control. Any page using these controls must also have the *SPSWC* tagprefix register tag added to the top of the page. The register tag is as follows:

```
<%@ Register Tagprefix="SPSWC" Namespace="Microsoft.SharePoint.Portal.WebControls"
Assembly="Microsoft.SharePoint.Portal, Version=14.0.0.0, Culture=neutral, PublicKeyToken=71e
9bce111e9429c" %>
```

Displaying Individual Properties

Which web control you use to display a profile property depends upon the type of data that you want to show. There are four options from which to choose.

The *ProfilePropertyCheckValue* Control

This control is used to conditionally show a property or a set of properties separated by text (such as a comma) that is specified as a variable in the control. For example, if you wanted to show the office followed by the office location separated by a comma, you would use the following code:

```
<SPSWC:ProfilePropertyCheckValue PropertyNames="Office,Location" runat="server" Text=", "/>
```

You can use any combination of string profile properties and whatever delimiting text that you want. If the value of one of the properties is null, this control will omit the delimiting text.

The *ProfilePropertyDisplayName* Control

This control is useful if you want to display the property name (for example, "Office: Human Resources" or "Location: Hong Kong SAR"). It will also pull the display name in the appropriate language, which is nice for making it work in cross-cultural scenarios. You use this control as follows:

```
<SPSWC:ProfilePropertyDisplayName PropertyName="Title" runat="server" />
```

The *ProfilePropertyImage* Control

As the name implies, this control is used to display images. It is primarily used to display the user's profile image. The image you see on the Overview page is *Large*. There are three other choices (*Small*, *Medium*, and *NotSet*). These are useful if you want to use the control on other pages. An example of the usage is as follows:

```
<SPSWC:ProfilePropertyImage PropertyName="PictureUrl" RenderWrapTable="False"
ShowPlaceholder="true" id="PictureUrlImage" ImageSize="Large" CenterVertically="true"
runat="server"/>
```

Notice that this control contains some other options, as well, like the *ShowPlaceHolder*. This displays the generic looking person icon; while not ideal, it is much better than a big X. This control is quite handy if you want to create a page that has a picture of a person. For example, if you create a form to allow managers to review a lot of employees, you could have the employee's picture display for immediate face recognition. Plus, it makes the form look a lot more professional.

The *ProfilePropertyValue* Control

This is the most commonly used profile control. It displays the value of the property for a given individual. It can be used for strings, numbers, HTML, URLs, and so on. It is best practice to encase these controls in <DIV> tags with classes so that you can apply styles to them (or hide them if they don't have values). An example of the usage for the Title field is shown here:

```
<SPSWC:ProfilePropertyValue PropertyName="Title" runat="server" ShowPrivate="True"
ApplyFormatting="True" PrefixBrIfNotEmpty="False" Font-Italic="True" TitleMode="False"/>
```

As with the other profile property controls, *ProfilePropertyValue* can be used on any SharePoint page, as long as the *ProfilePropertyLoader* control comes before it and you add the *SPSWC* tagprefix register to the top of the page. This can seriously jazz-up your pages if you are using profile information, and the profile properties can even be used to drive other applications by embedding the profile properties into URL strings. For example, you could build a URL string that passes an Employee ID to a Human Resources form. The form can then be pre-populated with the employee's profile information, saving the employee some typing and assuring standardization of the information provided.

The Edit Profile Page

The Edit Profile page is editprofile.aspx, and it is located in the LAYOUTS section of the SharePoint hive. One of the primary reasons this is changed is for data that is controlled outside of Active Directory or SharePoint in a third-party or custom application. If you plan to edit this page, you will want to make a backup (of course), and you will need to use some other tool than SharePoint Designer. As with all files in the _LAYOUTS directory that you change, the file must be consistently changed on all the servers in the farm that displays the web content. The control used by the Edit Profile page is *SPSWC:ProfileEditor*. There isn't a lot you can do with the control. If you want to remove or add fields you should do that by editing the profile property in Central Administration (Manage Service Applications | User Profile Service | Manage User Properties) and then select Edit from the drop-down menu next to the property's name) and selecting the Show On The Edit Details Page check box, as shown here in the following figure:

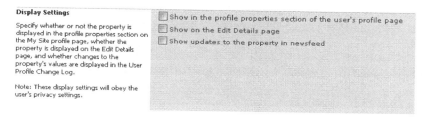

One item that you can't change is the activities that are followed. You need to do that another way, as described in the following section.

Hiding the Activities That I Follow

If you are not going to be using the News Feed or if you don't want users to be able to change what they are following, you can hide the News Feed section from the Edit Profile Page. By default, a user has many options, as shown here:

This large number of choices might be a little overwhelming to certain audiences, and there is definitely something to be said for simplifying things. It is a bit tricky to hide this section, but not too difficult. At first glance, it doesn't seem that you can hide the section at all. That is because you can't hide it without doing something else first which can be quite frustrating if you don't know the trick. That being said, you can avoid that frustration and simply follow these instructions to remove it:

1. Go to Central Administration.
2. Browse to the User Profile Service Application Page.
3. Click Manage User Sub-Types.
4. Create a new sub-type. It doesn't matter what you call it, because it will only be used to identify the items to hide. I usually choose "Activities Gone."
5. After you create the sub-type, you will want to go back to Manage User Properties.
6. Click the News Feed settings, and then click Edit.
7. Clear the Default User Profile Subtype check box, and then click OK.

   You will need to leave the one you created in the first part of this process selected.

That's all there is to it. The next time a user edits his profile, that section should be completely gone.

Editing Fields Outside of the User Profile Service

Often, you need to edit a field shown in your profile, but controlled by another data source (such as Active Directory or an HR system). These fields are typically items, such as telephone number, cube, address, or office. Normally, you fill out a form to make these changes happen, and these days the forms are most often online. The Edit Profile page is an excellent place to put the links to these forms. That way you only need to know how to get to one spot to make changes to all of your profile properties. You have a choice as to whether you want to put those links above or below the *SPSWC:ProfileEditor* control. To further consolidate the process, you can move the forms inside the SharePoint farm and convert them to InfoPath forms or simply normal SharePoint lists.

Chapter 7
Organizational Charts

The Organizational Charts (and I use the plural "charts" because they appear in multiple places) are all constructed based on information found in the Manager field of the data source used for profile synchronization. Normally, this is via Active Directory, but manager information can be brought in with a Business Data Service Connection. The most obvious and one of the coolest additions to Microsoft SharePoint 2010 is the Microsoft Silverlight Organizational Chart that appears on the Organization tab. The file for this page, OrganizationView.aspx, can be modified with SharePoint Designer 2010 by opening the My Site Host. There isn't a whole lot you can do to modify the Silverlight control, but you might want to modify the page if you are doing any branding so that the top part and the tabs look like they do on the other pages. That being said, we still have the Organizational Chart on the Overview page (person.aspx), and there is also an HTML version on the Organization tab if you don't like the Silverlight version (or don't have Silverlight installed). I think having an organizational chart on the Overview tab is overkill, because we have a whole tab dedicated to the Organizational Chart. Personally, I think that space could be used for a better purpose. I have used it for the My Links Web Part (the one that was in SharePoint 2007 but disappeared in SharePoint 2010) and for Twitter feeds. People really don't need multiple versions of the same chart, but at least the default setup has given us some options to work with.

Modifying the Silverlight Org Browser

The Silverlight control that displays the Organizational Chart is pretty well locked down, with no user-editable options. The control does have a style attached to it named *orgBrowser*. One of the things you can do with this style is to hide the HTML View option. This basically just makes the page look cleaner. The HTML version is available in two other places (Overview page and People Search) if people really want to see that. You can change the *orgBrowser* style by following performing these steps:

1. Open the My Site Host with SharePoint Designer 2010.

2. Click All Files.

3. Open organizationview.aspx by right-clicking the file, and then choosing Edit File In Advanced Mode.

4. Add the following style snippet inside of an asp:content tag.

```
<style type="text/css">
.orgBrowswer a:link{
display:none;
}
</style>
```

5. Save the file, and then you're done.

Replacing the Organizational Chart on the Overview Page

This section will show how to replace the Organizational Chart with the My Links Web Part. My Links was part of SharePoint 2007, and it was a great place to put links that were available within the SharePoint environment, regardless of which browser you use. A My Links Web Part was also included on the My Sites. You could choose to share the links with others or have them only appear for yourself. When you create a My Site Host in SharePoint 2010, you will notice the My Links are absent. That is because the emphasis is now on the Tag Cloud. While the Tag Cloud is nice, it takes some transition time for most users, and I believe the My Links functionality still has some value. Luckily, the My Links Web Part didn't really go anywhere. It is still available and you can use it on your pages. If you upgraded your content databases from an existing 2007 environment, then the links should still be there, too. Replacing the Organizational Chart on the Overview (person.aspx) page with the My Links Web Part is very easy and doesn't even require SharePoint Designer. Just follow these steps:

1. Browse to the Overview page (person.aspx) logged in as an account that can modify the page for everyone (for example, a site collection administrator).

2. Go to Site Actions | Edit Page.

3. Delete the existing Organizational Chart.

4. Click the Add A Web Part link that is right above the Web Part you deleted.

5. Choose the My Links Web Part from the available Web Parts, as shown in the following figure:

You should find it in the Recommended Items. If it is not found there, look in the Content Rollup section.

6. Modify the Web Part as you see fit, and then you're done.

The My Links will now work in a similar fashion to how they did in SharePoint 2007.

Chapter 8
Tags and Notes

Tags and notes are new to Microsoft SharePoint 2010. They represent some useful new features, but they also represent some new challenges to both the users and the administrators of SharePoint. In essence, a tag is just a word associated with a URL. You can use the tags feature to tie a number of URLs to specific keywords and then display them in a cloud on the tags and notes page. This is very similar to the "favorites" list on your browser, except tags are independent of the browser. In addition, they are indexed for search, and you can share them with other users. Notes fall under two categories: notes that are left for individuals on their My Site, and notes that are left on individual SharePoint pages.

Turning Tags and Notes Off

Not every organization wants to use tags and notes, and some might want to phase them in sometime after the initial introduction of SharePoint 2010. The settings for tags and notes are administered at the farm level. When the Managed Metadata Service (MMS) is enabled, tags and notes are turned on by default (the MMS is also a requirement for functionality). If you want to turn off tags and notes, you can do so with Windows PowerShell by using the following command:

```
Disable-SPFeature -Identity SocialRibbonControl
```

To turn it back on, use the following PowerShell command:

```
Enable-SPFeature -Identity SocialRibbonControl
```

The Tags And Notes link tied to the icon shown in the figure that follows will still seem to work if it was bookmarked in your browser, but the data will not be saved. This can result in some confusing behavior that needs to be addressed via training and/or communication. You can also use Farm Features in Central Administration to activate or deactivate the Social Tags

And Noteboard Ribbon Controls feature. Either one of these methods will affect the control that is in the upper-right corner with the Tag & Notes icons, as shown here:

If you turn off tags and notes, you should remove the thoughts.aspx page which displays your tags and notes from the My Site Host(s). You can do this by going to the Quick Links in the site settings of the My Site Host and then deleting the item that links to thoughts.aspx (the page is listed as _layouts/thoughts.aspx). This will remove the the tab with Tags & Notes and I Like It.

Enabling Tags and Notes for Individual Groups/Users

Tags and notes require certain permissions. These permissions can be controlled, thereby allowing or denying certain groups or individual users the ability to use these features. These permissions are located on the Central Administration's User Service Application page, which is located in the People section, as shown in the following:

The Permissions For Users dialog box opens, as shown here:

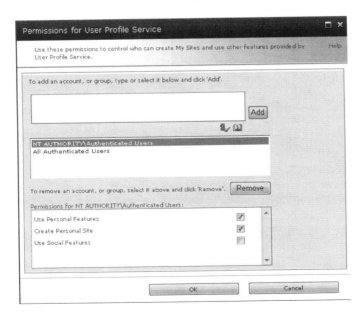

Here, you can manage three different areas of permissions regarding user profiles and social features. Select or clear the Use Social Features checkbox to control whether the user/group can use tags and notes. In the preceding screenshot, the permissions for Michael Doyle (me!) are set to be removed. You would think this would keep me from using tags and notes, but that would be incorrect. The permissions are additive. Because authenticated users have permissions to use Social Features (the default scenario when you create the User Profile Service), every authenticated user can use tags and notes no matter which group or users are added here. This makes paring out certain people from using the social features a lot harder. Most organizations have security groups that make the separation of users (for example, full time employees versus contractors) fairly straightforward. Just remember to remove the authenticated users (or turn off Use Social Features) to make the permissions work as they should.

Managing Tags and Notes

As of this writing, the only way to manage tags and notes is through Central Administration. An issue with the delete method in the object model has made it problematic for third-party vendors to create additional solutions. This leaves us with the interface that comes with SharePoint 2010. To go to the management page, navigate to your User Profile Service page, and then in the My Site Settings section, click Manage Social Tags And Notes, as shown in the following:

My Site Settings
Setup My Sites | Configure Trusted Host Locations | Configure Personalization Site | Publish Links to Office Client Applications | Manage Social Tags and Notes

The following dialog box opens, in which you can find and delete tags and notes:

An administrator might need to delete tags and notes if an employee leaves the organization, or if a tag or note contains wording that might be considered offensive language or sensitive information. While the item tagged might be security controlled, the tag itself is open to everyone.

You can enter one or more variables to bring back a list of tags and notes meeting the specified criteria. Your only option is to delete, and you are limited to viewing 100 items at one time; therefore, if you want to delete two thousand tags, you will need to repeat the process twenty times to delete all of them. This might not seem like a sizeable hurdle to overcome, but in a large organization, it is easy to see how this can be an administrative challenge. On the My Site Host page (thoughts.aspx) the user is limited to seeing 15 tags per keyword (by default).

Using PowerShell with Tags and Notes

The only PowerShell cmdlet that works with tags and notes is *Remove-SPSocialItemByDate*. This is a fairly limited cmdlet in that it only lets you remove tags, notes, and/or ratings before a given date. You specify which of the items you want and the date, but that is all. If you want to do anything else, you must use the interface in Central Administration. Use this cmdlet to clean out your database every once in a while to help increase the performance of your search indexing and free up disk space. Keep in mind that the items take very little space; thus it's more about search performance than the amount of space consumed, but it is still a good practice. The usage of the cmdlet is shown here.

Usage

```
Remove-SPSocialItemByDate -EndDate <DateTime> -ProfileServiceApplicationProxy
<SPServiceApplicationProxyPipeBind> [-AssignmentCollection <SPAssignmentCollection>]
[-Confirm [<SwitchParameter>]] [-RemoveComments <$true | $false>] [-RemoveRatings <$true |
$false>] [-RemoveTags <$true | $false>] [-SiteSubscription <SPSiteSubscriptionPipeBind>]
[-WhatIf [<SwitchParameter>]]
```

Argument Definitions		
EndDate	Required	The date specifying all items before it will be deleted.
ProfileServiceApplicationProxy	Required	The GUID of the User Profile Proxy.
AssignmentCollection	Optional	Can be used if you want to control object use and disposal.
Confirm	Optional	Asks you to confirm deletion before the command runs.
RemoveComments	Optional	If true, removes comments (notes).
RemoveTags	Optional	If true, removes tags.
RemoveRatings	Optional	If true, removes ratings.
SiteSubscription	Optional	Specifies account to run under. Mandatory in a hosted environment.
WhatIf	Optional	Display a message describing what would have happened if the command were run.

Example

```
Remove-SPSocialItemByDate -RemoveRatings $True -EndDate 11/1/2010
-ProfileServiceApplicationProxy 8582ebc9-bf37-46b6-a396-18d24070e39d
```

Note You can use the *Get-SPServiceApplicationProxy* cmdlet to retrieve the GUID of the Profile Service Application Proxy.

Chapter 9
Site Membership

You can see the sites and/or distribution lists of which a person is a member on the Memberships tab. This page (MyMemberships.aspx) is located in the _LAYOUTS directory of the Microsoft SharePoint hive, which makes it more challenging to modify because you cannot use SharePoint Designer to modify the file. Although it is nice to be able to see the sites of which a person is a member, there is an issue with the way this feature works. The only sites listed are those to which the user has been added explicitly; in other words, as an individual and not as part of a security group. Since almost everyone uses Active Directory security groups to manage site membership, you can see how this might cause some problems. Of course, the individual can add the site manually herself; this pretty much defeats the purpose of having a site list. The bright side to this is that if you are a member of hundreds (or in some case thousands) of sites, the page will not attempt to display all the site names.

Modifying the Page in SharePoint Designer

The MyMemberships.aspx page can be edited in SharePoint Designer with some modifications to the page. Logically, you will find it is much easier to make a page look like the other pages on your site if you use the same editing tool that you used for the other pages. SharePoint Designer is specifically designed to work with these pages, so it just makes sense to use it. The only issue is that you will need to return the modified page back to the _LAYOUTS directory; otherwise, the Edit Memberships will not work because it is hard-coded to look for that directory. You could modify the JavaScript, but that option is perhaps more complicated than necessary. To keep it simple, modify the page in SharePoint Designer and simply move the modified page back. To modify the Site Membership page in SharePoint Designer, perform the following steps:

1. Open your My Site Host in SharePoint Designer.

2. Create a new .aspx page.

   You can name it **MyMemberships.aspx** to keep things consistent. To open the newly created page, in Advanced Mode, click Edit File.

3. Log on to your SharePoint Server and browse to the _LAYOUTS directory.

4. Open MyMemberships.aspx in Notepad (or a similar program), and then copy all the text.

5. Paste the text in place of the code in the page that you created in step 2.

6. Remove the top two lines and store them someplace (for example, Notepad) to be used later. These will be the lines that begin with <%@ Page and <%@ Register.

7. In Advanced Mode, open person.aspx and take the top lines that begin with <%@ Page and <%@ Register. They should appear similar to the following:

```
<%@ Page language="C#" MasterPageFile="~masterurl/custom.master"
Inherits="Microsoft.SharePoint.Portal.WebControls.MySitePublicWebPartPage,Microsoft.
SharePoint.Portal,Version=14.0.0.0,Culture=neutral,PublicKeyToken=71e9bce111e9429c"
meta:progid="SharePoint.WebPartPage.Document" meta:webpartpageexpansion="full" %>

<%@ Register Tagprefix="SharePoint" Namespace="Microsoft.SharePoint.WebControls"
Assembly="Microsoft.SharePoint, Version=14.0.0.0, Culture=neutral,
PublicKeyToken=71e9bce111e9429c" %> <%@ Register Tagprefix="Utilities"
Namespace="Microsoft.SharePoint.Utilities" Assembly="Microsoft.SharePoint,
Version=14.0.0.0, Culture=neutral, PublicKeyToken=71e9bce111e9429c" %>

<%@ Register Tagprefix="WebPartPages" Namespace="Microsoft.SharePoint.WebPartPages"
Assembly="Microsoft.SharePoint, Version=14.0.0.0, Culture=neutral,
PublicKeyToken=71e9bce111e9429c" %> <%@ Register Tagprefix="OSRVWC"
Namespace="Microsoft.Office.Server.WebControls" Assembly="Microsoft.Office.Server,
Version=14.0.0.0, Culture=neutral, PublicKeyToken=71e9bce111e9429c" %>

<%@ Register Tagprefix="OSRVUPWC" Namespace="Microsoft.Office.Server.WebControls"
Assembly="Microsoft.Office.Server.UserProfiles, Version=14.0.0.0, Culture=neutral,
PublicKeyToken=71e9bce111e9429c" %>

<%@ Register Tagprefix="SPSWC" Namespace="Microsoft.SharePoint.Portal.WebControls"
Assembly="Microsoft.SharePoint.Portal, Version=14.0.0.0, Culture=neutral,
PublicKeyToken=71e9bce111e9429c" %>

<%@ Register Tagprefix="SEARCHWC"
Namespace="Microsoft.Office.Server.Search.WebControls"
Assembly="Microsoft.Office.Server.Search, Version=14.0.0.0, Culture=neutral,
PublicKeyToken=71e9bce111e9429c" %>

<%@ Register Tagprefix="PublishingWebControls"
Namespace="Microsoft.SharePoint.Publishing.WebControls"
Assembly="Microsoft.SharePoint.Publishing, Version=14.0.0.0, Culture=neutral,
PublicKeyToken=71e9bce111e9429c" %>

<%@ Register TagPrefix="wssuc" TagName="NavItem" src="/_controltemplates/NavItem.ascx"
%>
<%@ Register TagPrefix="wssuc" TagName="Welcome" src="/_controltemplates/Welcome.ascx"
%>
```

This will allow you to view the results of your changes in the browser.

8. Make all your changes with your new page in SharePoint Designer until you are satisfied with them.

9. When you are done making changes you can swap the top lines out again—that is, replace all the lines you copied from person.aspx with the original <%@ Page and <%@ Register lines from MyMemberships.aspx).

10. Copy the code from your SharePoint Designer file and put it into the one in the _LAYOUTS directory.

   You might want to create a new one, but if you do, you will need to modify the Quick Links on your My Site Host so that it points to the new file. If you keep the original file name, make copies of the newly created and the original files. Service Packs and upgrades could potentially write over any file in the _LAYOUTS directory.

That looks like a lot of steps, but it really isn't too hard once you have done it a few times. The main benefit is the shortening of development time when making branding-related changes.

Editing the Membership Control

The bad news is that there isn't much you can do with the Membership Control (the control called *MembershipMarcoView* on your .aspx page). The good news is that with a little JavaScript and cascading style sheets (CSS) you can change it around a bit. The problem is that it is an Active Server Page (ASP) control and not a standard Web Part, so we don't have the normal Web Part interface to use for making modifications. Furthermore, the text inside the control doesn't contains a CSS class that doesn't affect other items (columns use *ms-vb ms-srchAlignTop*, which is used by other controls). It's going to take a bit of fancy footwork on your part if you want to do anything with it.

As an example, take a look at the Show To column. There are five different options in the drop-down menu (Everyone, My Manager, My Team, My Colleagues, and Only Me), and the control has a TH class called *Privacy*. With that knowledge, you can hide it or do a variety of modifications to it that involve CSS. For this example, you're just going to hide the Show To column and take back the space that it uses. You use JavaScript to do this, but because you can't access the items directly, you'll need to identify them by *TagName* and content. By doing so, you can then assign them to a JavaScript variable that you can manipulate. You should place this code at the bottom of your page but still within the asp:content tag. The code to hide the column looks like this:

```
<script type="text/javascript">
//First hide the TH. This has the ID of Privacy so it is easy to get
var oPrivacy = document.getElementById("Privacy");
oPrivacy.innerText="";
//Next we want the items in the TD tag but we have to use the contents
//of the TD to determine which ones to hide.
var elem=document.body.getElementsByTagName("td");
//There are only five options so if we match one then we will set the
```

```
//innerText of the element to nothing.
for(var i=0;i<elem.length;i++)
{
        if(elem[i].innerText=="Everyone" || elem[i].innerText=="My Manager" ||
          elem[i].innerText=="My Team" ||
          elem[i].innerText=="My Colleagues" || elem[i].innerText=="Only Me")
{
 elem[i].innerText = "";
}
}
</script>
```

Once you have added this JavaScript, you'll have the space from that column, which will make the page look neater. This particular scenario is important if your collaboration model states that everyone can see anything that is added to the My Site Host. If you don't want a site membership shown to everyone, then you should remove the item. How you utilize these customizations will vary in accordance with your My Site philosophy, but this gives you the option to change some of the page behavior to meet the needs of your organization. If you wanted to do something similar with the Group Name column, you would use Group for the TH header and SharePoint Sites and Distribution Lists for the TD items to hide. While the degree of design flexibility of this control is limited, the example provided should give you enough information to get you started modifying the control itself.

Chapter 10
Colleagues

Colleagues are people you have chosen as your closest co-workers or associates at your organization. These are the people whose newsfeeds you want to follow. If you optionally make them part of your My Team, you might also provide them with additional permissions, such as read access to certain content on your profile. SharePoint will by default put your manager, all of the people on your team (those with the same manager), and people who work for you in your Colleagues, but you can choose to add or remove them. You can also think of Colleagues as your "friends" in a social network. The main incentive to actively manage your Colleagues is to throttle the items you see in your newsfeed. If you want to modify the Colleagues page (MyContactLinks.aspx) you must modify the file in the _LAYOUTS directory. As with all files in the _LAYOUTS directory, you will need to use another tool to modify it other than Microsoft SharePoint Designer 2010. If you do prefer to use SharePoint Designer 2010 (and I recommend this if you are going to be doing heavy modifications) the page can be temporarily placed in the My Site Host by using the same method used in Chapter 9, "Site Membership." The Colleagues page works with the newsfeed, but it can be safely removed from the My Site Host if you choose to do so. Reasons for this might be simplification of the My Site Host or that you have multiple My Site Hosts (such as a separate one for contractors). A new user will still have the default Colleagues given to them, but won't have access to the page that gives him the ability to add, modify, or delete Colleagues.

Suggested Colleagues

Microsoft Outlook 2010 has a SharePoint server Colleague add-in that scans the user's Sent Items folder for the names of people and words that are used often. It sends these users and words (potential keywords) to the SharePoint server hosting the user's My Site. When you click the View Suggestions link (this link appears on the Colleagues tab until a user adds a colleague from the suggested list, but it will come back after 15 days or 500 emails), you are presented with a list of these suggested users. Periodically (the default is monthly), SharePoint sends emails to people who have users in their suggested colleagues list and who have not updated their profiles recently. It will also send a list of keywords in the same email. Some people might consider this email as being intrusive because it is scanning their own emails, and they might wonder what other kind of information is being sent. You can stop this in several different ways:

- Disable the timer job
- Request that individuals disable the scan in Outlook 2010
- Disable the option through group policy
- Use the Office Customization Tool

Disabling the Timer Job

You can stop emails from being sent by disabling the timer job. The timer job that controls this is called User Profile Service – My Site Suggestions Email Job. To access the timer job, go to Central Administration, click Monitoring, and then under Timer Jobs, click Review Job Definitions. Timer jobs are listed alphabetically, so it will be toward the end of the list. This is probably my least favorite way of disabling those emails, but I often do it as a backup just to be completely assured that the emails are not sent. It also makes sense from an administrative standpoint, particularly if you are not going to send the information to SharePoint anyway. Keep in mind, however, that installing a Service Pack or implementing an upgrade can re-enable that timer job, as can running the SharePoint 2010 Products Configuration Wizard. This is the same job you would change if you want to change the frequency at which the emails are sent.

Turning Off Analysis of Emails

Turning off the email analysis feature is done via Outlook 2010. If the user doesn't have that version installed, the emails won't be scanned anyway. To disable this option, open Outlook, click File | Options, and then in the Outlook Options dialog box, select the Advanced option. Scroll down to the Other section and clear the check box for Allow Analysis Of Sent E-mails To Identify People You Commonly E-mail And Subjects You Commonly Discuss, And Upload This Information To The Default SharePoint Server, as shown in the following figure, and then click OK.

The wording of this option might seem a bit frightening to some people. I think the words "analysis of sent e-mails" makes people uneasy. Other social networks and search engines do similar types of analysis to improve search suggestions and advertisement targeting, but they don't call it out like that. People are getting more used to this kind of information scanning, but it can still send ripples through an organization. Any instructions sent to end users showing them how to disable this option should explain what information is being gathered and how it is being used. This will help them make a more informed decision.

Using Group Policy or Office Customization Tool

Using either of these tools is beyond the scope of the book, but you can refer to the TechNet article at *http://technet.microsoft.com/en-us/library/ff384821.aspx* for more information. I highly recommend the group policy method, because that is the cleanest way to remove email scanning from everyone that uses Outlook. You can get a little more specific in the settings if you use these tools, such as specifying the maximum number of recipients in an Outlook item to scan to determine the user's colleagues for recommendations, and the minimum time before starting Colleague recommendation scan. Obviously, you only care about those settings if you are going to keep the scanning active. The processing load is pretty minimal for this activity, but depending on the email load, you might want to modify the group policy to trim it down.

Chapter 11
Profile Properties

The profile properties determine the data that is used to represent a user. Some of this data will come from an external data source such as Active Directory, and some of it will be added by the user via the My Site user interface. No matter where the data comes from, the information is stored in the profile database (which by default is named *Profile DB*). You can add as many additional properties as you like, but I would recommend limiting them to those that make sense for your organization. Avoid any profile properties that might be seen as frivolous such as favorite movies or pet's name. In addition to the choice of which properties to display, consider the number of fields available. At some point, the addition of extra properties will be deemed by the user too much effort to fill out for the value the information provides. There are several properties included in the default My Site display; finding a place to put additional properties in a user-friendly viewing format is a challenge. Each profile property has a group of attributes that can be set at the time of property creation, and in some cases, modified after creation. Choosing the right properties is important and deserves some discussion. You can access the interface to manage user profile properties in Central Administration. Once there, click Manage Service Applications | User Profile Service | Manage User Properties.

Property Settings

The property attributes discussed in this section are the most important ones, because several of them (name, type, and length) cannot be altered once you have saved the property. If you decide a string needs to be longer at some point in the future, you must delete the property and recreate it. It is possible to export the data from the database manually and reimport it, but not without considerable effort. It is much easier to plan ahead as much as possible. The fields that come under the Property Settings are described in the subsections that follow.

Name

This field is used programmatically by the User Profile Service. It must be unique and cannot contain any spaces. It is also used any time you want to access the values of the property.

Display Name

This is a user-friendly name used to identify the property wherever it is found. It can be changed at any time without disrupting any of the related data. You can also add entries for different languages. To do this, click Edit Languages. For example, if you wanted to add the Spanish word for name (nombre), click Add Language, choose Spanish, and then enter **nombre** in the text box.

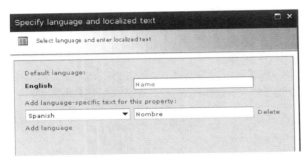

This is all that is needed to provide multilingual support for the user property. When the browser detects a different language preference, it will look for a match and display the proper description, if one is available.

Type

The data type is important to get right the first time. Choosing an improper data type can severely limit your ability to work with the data in the future. For example, if you use the Person type, you will be limited to choosing a single individual from your User Profile Service. There are several choices from which to choose:

- big integer
- binary
- boolean
- date
- date no year
- date time
- E-mail
- float
- HTML
- integer
- Person
- string (Multi Value)
- string (Single Value)
- time zone
- unique identifier
- URL

Most of these data types are self-explanatory, but the two string types are probably the most commonly used, and what makes them even more important is that they can be tied to term stores. If you can dedicate some time to creating a term store initially and some more time to maintaining it, this will greatly enhance the "findability" of your people search. Be careful choosing to have the term store closed when attaching it to user profile properties. With a closed term store, if the user types in something not found in the term store, they are presented with a pretty ugly and somewhat confusing error statement. This might discourage people from entering data. I think it is better to keep it open and have an administrator remove misspelled and inappropriate terms later, but that decision will vary with the needs of your organization.

Length

The Length setting defines the maximum number of characters that the data can be, and it is only available for data types for which it makes sense, such as string and HTML. You need to be aware that this setting cannot be changed once the property is created, it is better to have too many characters available than too few. If you aren't sure about the proper length for a property, then allow for some buffer and then add a little more. Length must be an integer between the values of 1 and 3600.

Multivalue Separator

You only have two choices for this one. You can choose commas or semicolons. You can also change it at any time. The change will take effect immediately for the values.

Configure a Term Set to be Used for this Property

Use of this setting enables the property to use a term store, and allows you to choose the term set from which keyword suggestions are made and where user-entered keyword additions are stored. This is a property that can be changed at a later date, so it isn't imperative that you choose a term store at the time of property creation. Where feasible, I recommend the use of a term store with profile properties, because doing so provides a wealth of managed metadata benefits and improves search performance.

Sub-Type of Profile

This property is useful if you want to have profile properties that display for specific groups of users (such as contractors or full-time employees), but not for others. It is also useful if you want to hide a user profile property from all users (such as the newsfeed options). One problem with this method is that if you want to hide a user profile property from use (but still keep it), then you must have at least two sub-types of profiles. If you clear the Default User Profile Type check box and you don't have another sub-type defined, you will get the following error when you try to save:

At least one sub-type must be selected.

Use this page to edit this property for user profiles.

* Indicates a required field

Once you have defined at least two sub-types, you can choose to have the user profile property not display in one of them. As the preceding figure states though, you must select at least one of the sub-types, as described in Chapter 6, "Modifying the My Site Host."

User Description

The User Description is the text that appears on the Edit Profile page that explains to the user what data the property is requesting, or provides an example of the proper format for data. As with the Display Name, you can enter different values for different languages. If you don't choose a default language, however, you will receive the following error:

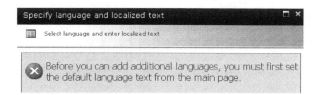

You shouldn't see this error if you have added a value for the Display Name, so be sure to add the Display Name value before adding the User Description. You can enter the values for any of the available languages and it will take effect, displaying the appropriate language, based on the browser properties.

Policy Settings

This group of property attributes controls how the user profile data is viewed and accessed by specific individuals and groups of people. These people include the user, the user's manager, colleagues, and everyone else. By modifying these settings, you are exposing or hiding the profile data. Care should be taken with this setting because sensitive information such as mobile phone numbers, employee IDs, and so on could potentially be exposed to anyone who can navigate to the My Site Host. That is because any program that can access web services and can navigate to the My Site Host URL can view user profile data (or at least those properties in the profile which are not specifically restricted from being viewed). The following subsections describe the attributes in this grouping in more detail.

Policy Setting

The name of this property is a little misleading. It basically comes down to whether the profile property is required, optional, or disabled. Setting a property to required simply means that the user cannot save the information entered on the Edit Details page without filling in something for this user profile property. Use the option to make items required sparingly. If a user spends a lot of time filling in the rest of the data but misses a required field, she will get an error message. Again, error messages such as this can contribute to a poor user experience and dissuade people from filling in the items. I recommend using training as a means to encourage users to fill in their data, rather than making fields required. Disabled means that users cannot edit the field at all, but all previously entered data is still retained and displayed.

Default Privacy Settings

This field determines who by default can actually see the value of this profile property, regardless of how it is accessed. The options are Only Me, My Manager, My Team, My Colleagues, and Everyone. The only group not well defined here is My Team, which includes everyone who has the same manager (and the manager, too). You should try to keep it simple; unless there is a compelling business reason to limit the default settings, then stick with Everyone. That will make training easier, and people will know that whatever they put into their My Sites will be visible to everyone else in the organization.

User Can Override

This setting is used in conjunction with the Default Privacy Settings. When selected, it allows users concerned about the data privacy to choose the Default Privacy Settings themselves. This is a good option if you have users with special privacy concerns, because it gives users some control over the visibility of their data.

Replicable

Select this option if you want the data to replicate to the User Information List, which is a hidden list that resides in every site collection. It consists of everyone who has navigated to the site collection or who has been manually added as an individual to the site permissions. Even though storing this information at the site collection level might seem redundant, it is mainly used to display user information regarding document modification and discussion posts in farms that don't use My Site Hosts. It will also display information for people who have left the organization (and therefore are no longer in the user profile store) but whose information might remain useful in the site collection(s) because they authored or changed some content. The only way you can delete individuals from the User Information List is by doing so manually.

Edit Settings

This grouping is for setting whether or not a user can update the information in the property. This is done for data that is normally controlled by Active Directory, data that is controlled by an external source, or data that the organization has decided should only be updated by a system administrator or designated person. For example, company policy might state that only the official employee photo should be used as a profile picture. Using the setting Do Not Allow Users To Edit Values For This Property prevents users from changing the picture to an avatar or snapshot. Basically, you need to decide who owns the data and if users can be trusted to update it.

Display Settings

This set of properties determines where the data is displayed (user profile page, edit details page, and newsfeed). The Policy Settings determine who sees the data, regardless of the Display Settings.

Show In the Profile Properties Section of the User's Profile Page

The user's profile page is person.aspx (by default) in the My Site Host. If this check box is selected for a profile property, the property will be available on that page. If you want it to display without having to use the drop-down list on the page, you must manually add it the page by using Microsoft SharePoint Designer (or a similar tool). If you do this, the setting doesn't matter, because it will show up as long as the viewer has permission to see it.

Show on the Edit Details Page

This option needs to be selected if you want users to update the value of the user profile property. You might also want to display values for the user's sake (such as employee ID). In addition, you will want to select this if you selected the User Can Override check box in the Policy Settings.

Show Updates to the Property in Newsfeed

Select this option if the property is something that should appear in the newsfeed. There are already a lot of items in the newsfeed as it is, so avoid adding items unless there is a good reason to do so. The more items, the more irrelevant each one becomes in the eye of the user. That being said, when there is a definitive need, there isn't much additional overhead in adding more items.

Search Settings

This setting controls how the user profile property is indexed during a people search crawl. These settings affect the ability to use Search to find people in an efficient manner. If you change items in these settings, you will need to do a full people search crawl before they take effect.

Alias

This is for properties that represent the user uniquely, such as the logon name. For example, if one of the properties is *EmployeeId*, a user could type this property in the search box and it would bring back documents associated with the person just as if you typed the name of the person. Given that few properties contain data that is truly unique to a user, there should only be a few items for which this property is selected.

Indexed

Select this check box if you want the property to be searched. An example would be office location. If you want to be able to bring back everyone located in a certain office by searching, you would need to ensure that it is indexed.

Property Mapping for Synchronization

You can modify or delete any entries that might have been added. For most mappings you will just be able to delete. The data will remain the same until the next profile synchronization. You will want to run a full profile import on the relevant profile connection. You can only have one mapping per user profile property.

Add New Mapping

This is where you would add an item from the profile connections (such as an Active Directory connection). Once you do the first synchronization, you can choose the property to map to. If you have more than one Data Source Connection, you will need to choose the one you want. New in SharePoint 2010 is the Export option (in addition to the Import option). You can only choose one direction though. With the Export option, you have self-service for some of their Active Directory fields. A good example of this is letting users update their own mobile phone number similar to how users can send their profile pictures to Active Directory, as described in Chapter 13, "Outlook Integration."

Using Profile Properties with Twitter

You can use profile properties to feed person-specific values onto a page. A great example of this is the Twitter widget. With the combination of user profile values and the publicly available Twitter widget, you can display a person's Twitter feed on their profile page. It is pretty simple as long as you have the few snippets of JavaScript and HTML and a little guidance. The steps that follow outline how to do this, but first you will need to decide where you want the Twitter feed to go. One good spot is on the profile page (person.aspx). That way, when you view the person's profile you will see their Twitter feed. I recommend replacing the organizational chart because it is redundant and takes up about the same amount of space. To show the Twitter feed, you need to obtain some script from Twitter, modify it with a little JavaScript, create and populate the profile property, and then modify the .aspx page in the My Site Host, as follows:

1. Go to *Twitter.com*.

2. At the bottom of the page, click Resources.

3. In the Widgets section, click See All Widgets.

   A page opens, presenting a list of widgets

4. Choose the widget for My Website.

5. Choose the Profile Widget.

   This is the one that displays a list of Twitter updates. Provide a Twitter account name to use as a sample for the display customization.

6. You can now customize the look and feel of your widget.

   There are four sections (Settings, Preferences, Appearance, and Dimensions). Modify these until the widget looks the way you want. You might want to adjust the color options to better match your site theme.

7. Click Finish & Grab Code to get the JavaScript code; store it in Notepad temporarily (or just leave the page open so you can copy it later).

8. Open the My Site Host in SharePoint Designer.

9. Create a text file in Site Assets with an appropriate name, such as **twitter.txt**.

10. Paste the widget code in the newly created text file, and then save it.

11. Open person.aspx (or whichever page you are modifying) and insert a Content Editor Web Part where you want the Twitter feed to be located.

If the Web Part does not show up, you can add it by clicking Site Actions | Site Settings | Web Parts in the Galleries section. You will need to click New, and then select the check box next to Microsoft.SharePoint.WebPartPages.ContentEditorWebPart. Click Populate Gallery, and then refresh the page or SharePoint Designer and it will show up.

12. Edit the Web Part and point to the newly created text file by using the Content Link property.

13. Verify that the script works. Once you have stopped editing the page, the Twitter feed for the account you used when you created the widget should be displayed.

14. Go to Central Administration. Create a new profile property by using the String data type in the User Profile Service application from the Manage User Properties screen.

Ensure that the check box for Show On Edit Details page is selected if you want users to be able to update their own properties. (I used the name TwitterHandle, but you can name the property whatever you want, so long as the name does not contain spaces.) If you use a different property name, be sure to change the appropriate spots in the code.

15. Populate the property for one of the users you will use for testing.

16. In SharePoint Designer, in Advanced Mode, edit the page where you placed the widget. Switch to the Code view. Place the following snippet right below the *SPSWC:ProfilePropertyLoader* tag. This will put the value of the *TwitterHandle* property on the page but hide it.

```
<div id="divTwitterHandle" style="display:none">
<SPSWC:ProfilePropertyValue PropertyName="TwitterHandle" runat="server"
ShowPrivate="True" ApplyFormatting="True" PrefixBrIfNotEmpty="False"
Font-Italic="True" id="TwitterHandle" TitleMode="False"/>
</div>.
```

17. Open the widget code in the text file you created earlier, and then add the following lines below the second <script> tag.

```
//get the object so it can be manipulated
var obj = document.getElementById("divTwitterHandle");
//obtain the value of the profile property
var sTwitterHandle = obj.innerText;
//Get rid of the space at the end of the text
sTwitterHandle = sTwitterHandle.replace(/\s+/g,'');
```

18. Go to near the bottom of the text file and find the line with `.render().setUser` in it. Replace the hard-coded user name (for example, SharePointNinja) with the variable *sTwitterHandle* so that it looks like this.

```
}).render().setUser(sTwitterHandle).start();
```

19. Save your file and you are done.

You might want to put in to some additional handling for people who don't use Twitter (for example, make the web part hide itself), or you can leave it as is.

That is all you need to do! Now individuals can view other user's Twitter feeds by going to their My Site, as long as the user has populated his user profile property correctly.

Chapter 12
People Search

The people search page is part of the Enterprise Search Center. It is a lot like a normal results page, except that, as its name implies, it returns only people in the search results, and the results are formatted with a people results-specific XSL. One of the most significant and useful changes to people search is that it now searches phonetically. This means it will return results that sound similar (for example, a search on Steve will bring back Steve, Steven, Stephen, and Stephanie). This is extremely helpful if a user doesn't know the exact spelling of a person's name. Another benefit is the Refinement panel. You can you this panel to filter the search results, based on attributes such as title or office location. All of this functionality is available without any special configuration. People search is great out of the box, but there might be times when you want to customize it.

People Refinement Panel

The Refinement panel (which appears on the left side of the window) is key to whittling down your results. It is a great tool out of the box, but with some minor modifications, you can make it even more powerful. The following illustration shows the Refinement category found in the Modify Web Parts section of the People Refinement Panel Web Part.

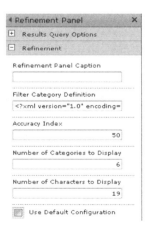

You might have noticed that the Number Of Categories is set to 6, but you are probably only seeing four refinement options on the people search page. This means that the Use Default Configuration check box is selected (it is not selected in the figure). That is how it is configured out of the box, and if you don't clear this check box, then nothing you change in this configuration will take effect.

Refinement Panel Caption

This caption is used to display information in addition to the chrome text (this is the text that appears in the title box of the web part). It appears above the refinement options and can be used to provide some clarifying text, such as "Click on an item below to refine your search" or anything else that might be useful.

Filter Category Definition

To add additional filter categories, add the category here, following the same XSL pattern as the existing categories. The easiest way to do this is to copy one of the categories from the text and modify it. An example is presented in the following:

```
<Category    Title="Education"    Description="Use this filter to restrict results by
Education" Type="Microsoft.Office.Server.Search.WebControls.ManagedPropertyFilterGenerator"
MetadataThreshold="1"    NumberOfFiltersToDisplay="15"    MaxNumberOfFilters="0"
SortBy="Frequency"    SortByForMoreFilters="Name"    SortDirection="Descending"
SortDirectionForMoreFilters="Ascending"    ShowMoreLink="True"    MappedProperty="Education"
MoreLinkText="show more"    LessLinkText="show fewer"    />
```

In the preceding sample, there are already a number of categories. Unfortunately, the built-in text editor is a little difficult to work with, and it's easy to make mistakes. So, you'll probably find it easiest to copy the text into something like Notepad, make your modifications, and then copy the text back into the text box. Any mistake in formatting can make the whole control fail. A backup is handy but not essential because you can copy the text from another Refinement panel. The most important attributes are the *Title* and the *MappedProperty* (the name of the user profile property). Again, make sure the Use Default Configuration check box is cleared, or your changes will not take effect.

The filter categories display in the order in which they appear in the definition. If you want to ensure that a certain type of filter appears every time, place the category so that its placement in the list is within the number of categories to display. For example, if you are displaying six categories, list the filter category within the first six categories in the definition.

Counts of the results returned are turned off by default. To show count results for your categories, you must add the *ShowCounts* property to each categories for which you want to display a count, as shown in the following example (make sure the quotes are regular straight quotes and not curly quotes):

```
ShowCounts= "Count"
```

Add this attribute to the end of the category tag, just before the closing "/>" characters. Once you have added the attribute, the count will display to the right of the fields returned in the category.

Finally, if you select the Use Default Configuration check box, all of your changes will be overwritten. I recommend either turning on versioning for the document library where the modified page is stored, or saving the field text to a separate text file and putting it in another document library or in a safe location.

Accuracy Index

This property determines how many values to base the filters on. For example, if your search returns 1,000 results, only the first 50 (by default) will be used to determine the categories. It will also be used to determine the counts. This can be deceiving to the user if the number of counts returned is much less that the obvious number of results. Be careful making this number too high; if your organization uses Search frequently or if there are a large number of searches that return thousands or even millions of items, a high accuracy index can affect performance. Increased values require increased amounts of CPU power and more time to return results. It requires some real world testing to establish a value that works for your particular environment.

Number of Categories to Display

The Number of Categories to Display is the maximum number of categories that will be displayed. Depending on the number of results returned, you might see a smaller number of categories. The decision on how many categories to use is based upon how you want the page to appear. It is also limited by the number of categories that are defined in the Filter Category Definition field. Most implementations typically settle for six. If you use more categories than that, the refinement panel might format it as two columns, pushing everything to the right.

Number of Characters to Display

The default for the number of characters to display is 16. If your refinement item is longer than that, it will display with an ellipse (...) appended to the end. This seems a little short so you should do some testing to determine what works best for your organization. Titles, for instance, are usually much longer than 16 characters. Depending on your organization's typical screen resolution, you can probably go up to 30 characters without causing user interface issues.

Modifying the People Results

The People Results page is a specially modified version of the search core results. It only shows users, and it can be an effective replacement for an employee directory. Modifying the results page is not easy. The XSL that transforms the results is over 600 lines. I don't recommend doing major alterations unless you are willing to spend some time and either you or someone in your organization is familiar with modifying XSL (or is willing to put in the time to learn); it is difficult for beginners or people that don't use it on a regular basis to make modifications in a timely manner. If you do want to modify the people search results, I have provided some guidance to get you started. In the example that follows, you will learn how to remove a link.

Removing the Add To My Colleagues Link

To remove the Add To My Colleagues link, follow these steps:

Caution Before undertaking any changes, make a backup of any XSL file that you plan to modify, or put version control on the page. If you use Microsoft SharePoint Designer 2010 to edit search pages, be aware that it has a tendency to overwrite the XSL Link property. Also, if you don't see the results take effect, you might want to create an XSL file for the facets Web Part, as well. I have seen some erratic behavior result from modifying the facets control; to correct this, you might need to copy and create a new XSL file, even if you don't modify the copied XSL.

1. Log on as an account with edit permission, and then open the Search Center People Results page in the browser.

2. Click Site Settings | Edit Page.

3. Scroll down to the People Core Results Web Part and choose Edit This Web Part from the drop-down list.

   The People Search Core Results panel appears in the upper-right. You might need to scroll upward to see it.

4. Expand the Display section, clear the Use Location Visualization check box, and then click XSL Editor to view the current XSL code, as shown in the following figure.

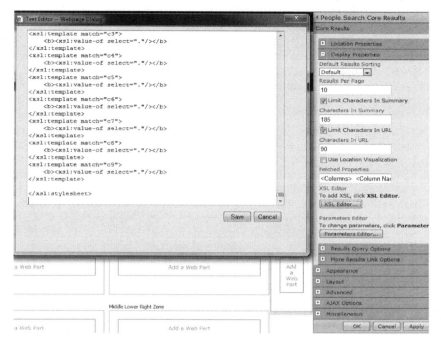

5. To remove the Add As A Colleauge link, remove the following lines of code from the XSL file:

```
<xsl:if test="$hasacu">
  <li id="AddColleagueLinkField">
  <a id="{concat($currentId, '_AddColleagueLink')}"
  href="{ddwrt:EnsureAllowedProtocol(string(addtomycolleaguesurl))}">&#187;
<xsl:value-of
  select="$AddToMyColleaguesText" /></a>
  </li>
  </xsl:if>
```

6. Save the file to a location within the Site Center such as Site Assets, with a logical name such as **XSLModified.aspx**.

7. Copy the URL to the file.

8. Expand the Miscellaneous section, and then paste the URL to the XSLModified.aspx file in the XSL Link field.

9. Click OK, and then click Save and Close.

Chapter 13
Outlook Integration

My Site data can greatly enhance the Microsoft Outlook experience by providing profile information such as newsfeed items and profile pictures that shows you a photo of every recipient of the your email. This gives instant visual recognition of who is on the email thread, which can help the user to identify its relative importance. The My Site Outlook Social Connector provides a view into the My Site of any person who sends you an email (if they have a My Site that you can access). Outlook 2010 provides the greatest amount of integration, but most of the functionality is available in Outlook 2007, as well. Outlook interacts with SharePoint in a variety of ways not related specifically to My Sites, such as integrated calendars, offline viewing of document libraries, and email-enabled libraries. This section does not cover these items, but it is good to be aware of them, because My Sites are still Microsoft SharePoint sites, and there are some definite benefits to these tools, especially for personal sites.

Outlook 2010 includes a feature that scans emails and sends information about possible colleagues and keywords to SharePoint. SharePoint then periodically sends emails to users containing these suggestions. Scanning of emails can be considered intrusive by some organizations and probably will be opposed by at least some of the users. This setting is enabled by default, so you might want to disable this for some or all of your users. The options that you can use to disable this feature are covered in more detail in Chapter 10, "Colleagues."

The Outlook 2010 Social Connector for My Sites

Outlook 2010 comes with an option to connect to various sites that contain social data. The only connector built into Outlook is the one that connects to SharePoint My Sites. You can also download other connectors, such as the connectors for Facebook, Windows Messenger, and MySpace. We will focus on the connector for SharePoint My Sites, but it is important to know about the others, because Outlook will combine them so that the data from all the installed social connectors appears in the same location. This means newsfeeds from Facebook might push down newsfeeds (and other items) from SharePoint because it is a first-in, first-out scenario. Additionally, there is not a lot of control over how the data is consumed and presented. Any user that can install programs on their machine can install these additional social connectors. The best solution is to inform and train your users so that they can make appropriate decisions. You will also need to provide some instructions for your users on how to configure the SharePoint My Sites connector, as discussed in the following subsections.

Configuring the My Site Social Connector

To configure the My Site Social Connector, perform the following:

1. Open Outlook 2010.

2. Click View | People Pane | Account Settings.

3. Select the My Site check box in the Microsoft Outlook dialog box. Note that you will not see the Facebook connection if you have not installed it.

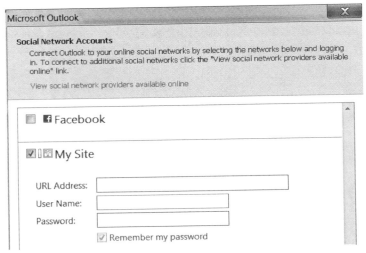

4. Type in the URL address of the My Site host and your User Name and Password. You will also need to update the Password every time you change it.

5. Click Connect.

You will now see My Site newsfeeds of the people who send you email in the People pane (as long as the People pane is on). You won't see results right away. It can take up to an hour or so before you see newsfeed items. Outlook will poll the My Site Host periodically for updates. There are also a couple of settings for the Social Connectors. These settings affect all the Social Connectors. The settings are related to how you want your contacts updated (automatically, with prompting, or never) and how long do you want to keep the newsfeed items (an important consideration, since it uses local storage). To access these options, click the Settings button at the bottom of the Social Network Accounts dialog box. The Settings dialog box opens, as shown in the following figure:

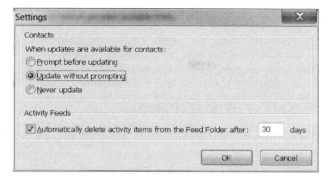

That is all you need to do to connect Outlook to My Sites!

Referring back to the Social Network Accounts dialog box, you might have noticed the View Social Connectors Available Online link. You can use this to obtain other social connectors. While many companies probably wish they could remove that link, currently, there is no way to hide this option.

Turning Off the Social Connector Add-In

If you don't want the social connector option to appear at all, you can turn off the Add-In from Outlook. You must be an administrator to completely remove it, but you can turn it off by performing the following instructions:

1. Open Outlook 2010.

2. Click File | Options, and then choose Add-Ins.

3. At the bottom of the dialog box, verify that the drop-down list next to Manage displays Com Add-Ins, and then click Go.

4. Clear the Microsoft Outlook Social Connector check box. This will remove the People Pane icon from the Outlook menu.

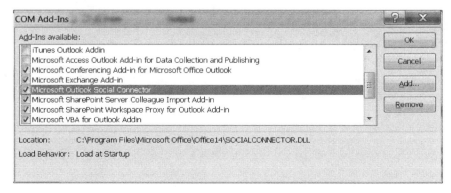

5. Click OK to finish up.

You can always add the Microsoft Outlook Social Connector by using the same interface. If you have administrator rights you can remove it altogether (so that it doesn't show up on the list). This might come in handy if you are responsible for setting up computers (such as temporary configurations for contractors).

Showing the My Site Photos in Outlook

If you have more than one social connector installed, you will have noticed that those other than the My Site connector show the profile picture of the person. Most companies seem to want it the other way around, with Outlook displaying the My Site photo and suppressing the pictures from other sites. At the moment, that isn't possible, but you can get Outlook to display the photo from the user's My Site. Outlook can use the *thumbnailPhoto* attribute from Active Directory (AD), and SharePoint 2010 can write to AD instead of just reading from it (provided the account used to synchronize the User Profile Service with AD has proper permissions). This means that with a little configuration, you can display My Site photos in Outlook (and what a great way to get people to update their profile pictures). To do this, perform the following:

1. Browse to the User Profile Service in Central Administration, and then in the People section, choose Manage User Properties.

2. Select the Picture property, and then click Edit.

3. Scroll down to the bottom of the screen to the Add New Mapping section.

4. In the Source Data Connection drop-down list, select the Active Directory data sources (for example, Active Users or whatever you named it).

5. From the Attribute drop-down, select thumbnailPhoto.

6. From the Direction drop-down, select Export.

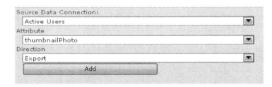

7. Click Add, wait for it to finish, and then click OK.

8. Go back to the User Profile Service page and click Start Profile Synchronization.

9. Choose Start Full Synchronization, and then click OK.

Wait for the synchronization to finish. The profile pictures should show up in Outlook for the My Site users in your organization. If they don't, verify data is being sent to AD; if the pictures are not in AD, the problem is likely due to a lack of permission to write to AD. If the pictures are in AD but not displaying in Outlook, the problem is most likely with Microsoft Exchange. Once the pictures have been sent from SharePoint to AD, then SharePoint has completed its task and does not interact directly with Outlook regarding the photos.

Chapter 14
Personal Sites

Personal Sites are the personal space for the users of the My Site Host. Some organizations might choose not to implement personal sites, but these sites offer a lot of benefits and give users a place to call their own in the organization. Users can place both shared documents as well as personal documents in a space that is regularly backed up and available from any computer on the network. The biggest issue with personal sites is that they are each their own site collection. This means that for every personal site, you have a site collection administrator and everything that comes with a site collection, such as groups, master pages, themes, galleries, sites, and so on. For the most part this doesn't really present a problem, because most users don't know enough about changing Microsoft SharePoint to cause problems, but with the adventuresome user, administering these sites can be a headache for your Help Desk staff. There is also the issue of branding; there simply isn't an easy way to apply branding standards across so many site collections (in some cases, thousands). But it can be done, and this chapter explains how. With some careful thinking and a little bit of work, personal My Sites can be a useful and integrated part of your intranet.

Keeping the Master Page Consistent

Most organizations would like to maintain a consistent user interface, or at least start with a master page that includes some branding. You could change the site definition, but this can be fairly problematic and does nothing to help you if you have personal site collections already in place.

Replacing the Default Master Page with a Custom Master Page

Luckily, you can create a feature with code that will replace the default master page with a custom master page. You can even use Windows PowerShell to activate the feature across all the personal site collections. This doesn't keep the individual user from changing their master page to something else, but this will be sufficient for almost all users. The detailed process of creating, building, and deploying features in Microsoft Visual Studio is beyond the scope of this book. If you are unfamiliar with feature creation and deployment, you should enlist the help of a developer experienced with SharePoint solutions to create the feature file for you with the provided code. Don't feel as if you are tied to this solution. This is just one that works for me, and I have found it to be a very slick solution that has turned a rather troublesome problem into an opportunity to brand thousands of SharePoint sites.

Step 1: Create the Master Page

On a personal site collection (your own or a test that you have set up), modify the master page via SharePoint Designer. If the account used has editing permission for the My Site Host, choose a personal page such as My Content to avoid making changes to the My Site Host master while it is in use. Ensure that any cascading style sheets (CSS) or image files are available from a common location such as the My Site Host. Once you are done modifying the master page, save the file to an external location that you can access later. This will end up being the master file applied to all the site collections, but it will be loaded inside a module of the feature, and will be loaded by the feature into the Master Page directory on the SharePoint server.

Step 2: Create a Solution

Create a solution that can be deployed to a farm. I recommend using at least Visual Studio 2010, because the integration with SharePoint has been greatly enhanced. Choose an Empty SharePoint Project and scope it at the site collection level. This solution will have two major parts. The first part will be placing the master page you created in Step 1 in a code module in the solution. The second part will be an event receiver based upon activating a feature.

Step 3: Add a Module

In your newly created solution, add a module. Right-click the newly created module, add a new folder, and then place your master page file in that folder. It should look similar to the following figure (depending on what you named the items):

Step 4: Add a Feature with an Event Receiver

This step is very important. Inside the feature, you will create an event receiver that will fire the code upon feature activation or deactivation. First, add a feature to your solution, right-click the feature, and then choose Add Event Receiver, as shown in the following figure:

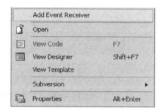

Once you have added the event receiver, you need to add some code. Visual Studio 2010 provides some commented out code to get you going, if you want to write your own, or you can use the code provided here.

Step 5: Put the Code in the Event Receiver

Add the following code to the event receiver. Once the code is added, you can build your solution and deploy it.

```
using System;
using System.Runtime.InteropServices;
using System.Security.Permissions;
using Microsoft.SharePoint;
using Microsoft.SharePoint.Security;

namespace MyMaster.Features.MySite
{
    // The GUID attached to this class may be used during packaging
    // Create your own GUID and replace the one here
    [Guid("fd9ba37c-3fb2-4b44-abe4-fd36ec6d5ecf")]

    // This is the event receiver that will be fired when the feature is activated
    // It swaps out the current master pages for the one in the directory of your
    // feature. In this case masterpage/NewMySiteMaster.master
    public class WEMySiteEventReceiver : SPFeatureReceiver
    {
        public override void FeatureActivated(SPFeatureReceiverProperties properties)
        {
            using (SPSite curSite = (SPSite)properties.Feature.Parent)
            {
                using (SPWeb curWeb = curSite.RootWeb)
                {
                    //Create a full master url
        Uri masterUri = new Uri(curWeb.Url +
        "/_catalogs/masterpage/NewMySiteMaster.master");
                    //all form/pages not publishing
                    curWeb.MasterUrl = masterUri.AbsolutePath;
                    //publishing pages
```

```
                curWeb.CustomMasterUrl = masterUri.AbsolutePath;
                curWeb.Update();
            }
        }
    }

    // This is the event that fires when the feature is deactivated. It replaces the
    // site's master page with mysite.master. This is because mysite.master should
    // always be there.
    // This may not be true in future versions of SharePoint, which may have
    // a different default master page. If you plan to use this code in a web
    // app not hosting sites, change this to v4.master. Again, this file name is subject
    // to change in later version of SharePoint.

    public override void FeatureDeactivating(SPFeatureReceiverProperties properties)
    {
        using (SPSite curSite = (SPSite)properties.Feature.Parent)
        {
            using (SPWeb curWeb = curSite.RootWeb)
            {
                //Create a full master url
                Uri masterUri = new Uri(curWeb.Url +
                "/_catalogs/masterpage/mysite.master");
                //all form/pages not publishing
                curWeb.MasterUrl = masterUri.AbsolutePath;
                //publishing pages
                curWeb.CustomMasterUrl = masterUri.AbsolutePath;
                curWeb.Update();
            }
        }
    }
}
```

Step 6: Deploy the Solution

Once you have built the solution and it is error free, deploy it to the farm and activate it on the web application that contains the My Site Host. Simply deploying the solution will not do anything but make the feature available on the site collection. You will still need to activate the feature.

Step 7: Activate the Feature Across the Personal Site Collections

You will most likely have a number of personal site collections in place when you deploy the solution, and manually activating the feature on each site collection will be time prohibitive. Don't worry, you can use PowerShell to iterate through each site collection and activate the feature. The process is amazingly quick and can be run via a timer job or part of an event receiver, based on site creation. To activate the feature, open the PowerShell console as an account with SP-ShellAdmin privileges, and then type the command that follows, replacing

$WebAppNameorURL with the URL of the My Site Host and $FeatureIdOrName with the name of the feature you created.

```
Get-SPSite -Limit ALL -WebApplication $WebAppNameorUrl |%{    Enable-SPFeature
$FeatureIdOrName -url $_.Url }
```

This will activate the feature and swap out the master page. If you start with the top level of the My Site Host, it will change the master page of the host, which will affect all current and future My Sites using that host. If you do that and want to change it back, deactivate the feature, and then change the master page to what you want by using SharePoint Designer. You can also turn on publishing (temporarily) and then change the master page via the site settings.

Index

About the Author

 **Michael Doyle** started his IT career nearly twenty years ago as a programmer for Federal Express Corporation (now FedEx). Since then, he has had the opportunity to work for corporate icons such as Intel, HCA, and Deloitte, as well as the United States Navy. For the last eight years, he has worked almost exclusively with Microsoft SharePoint in various capacities. He can be found speaking at SharePoint conferences around the world and throughout the United States or blogging and tweeting under the SharePoint Ninja name, which rose from the early days of SharePoint when it was much harder to find information about the product and many of the solutions required esoteric knowledge. (Luckily, knowledge is now more freely available thanks to the ever-widening SharePoint community.) When he isn't working with SharePoint, he can be found spending time outdoors, kayaking, hiking, diving, or finding any excuse he can to enjoy nature.

What do you think of this book?

We want to hear from you!
To participate in a brief online survey, please visit:

microsoft.com/learning/booksurvey

Tell us how well this book meets your needs—what works effectively, and what we can do better. Your feedback will help us continually improve our books and learning resources for you.

Thank you in advance for your input!

CPSIA information can be obtained at www.ICGtesting.com
Printed in the USA
BVOC010127020512

289192BV00003B/2/P

9 780735 6620